Jesus in Jail

Joy Dutton-Seltzer

TEACH Services, Inc.
P U B L I S H I N G
www.TEACHServices.com • (800) 367-1844

Copyright © 2019 Joy Dutton-Seltzer
Copyright © 2019 TEACH Services, Inc.
ISBN-13: 978-1-4796-1124-9 (Paperback)
ISBN-13: 978-1-4796-1125-6 (ePub)
Library of Congress Control Number: 2019915999

TEACH Services, Inc.
P U B L I S H I N G
www.TEACHServices.com • (800) 367-1844

Dedication

Lewis Martin Swinney

John Lewis Green Swinney

My dad and his dad

Table of Contents

Foreword

As a sanguine, loving person needing to hug and have conversation with anyone who "was there" in my space, I thought that PEOPLE were my only source of JOY. But once I discovered SOLITUDE, I embraced solitude, and my loneliness dissolved, disappeared—POOF!

It could be that loneliness is your best friend. It worked out that way for me. Many years of deep loneliness put me on a path into delightful SOLITUDE.

Prison is a place of solitude, and my hope is that you, too, can come to see that as a blessing.

But prison is also a place of isolation. There were two events in my life that showed me what isolation looked like and gave me a heart for those who find themselves in prison.

While visiting my neighbor Bob in prison, once each month for nine years, I observed the many reactions of those in the large visiting room. During those visits, Bob's wife and his young daughter and I became good friends over the years.

How shattered we all were that Bob had been incarcerated. As the long Sunday afternoons would drag on, we usually included God in our conversations.

Bob and his wife are Jews, and I'm a Christian. But as neighbors, we had a special bond.

I looked around in the visiting room from time to time; there were about 100 people there. I realized that most of the other inmates had no one visiting them.

Emotions run high on a visiting day, and PEACE is usually NOT one of those emotions. Yet, as the months and years passed, acceptance and a certain peace prevailed with Bob and his family.

After Bob's release from prison, I moved away and did not see them again.

Several years later, I met JoAnn, who was the editor of "By Beholding We Become…," a prison newsletter for inmates in Arizona. JoAnn happened to have been one of my students years ago in the Phoenix area, and so we were already friends.

When she explained about her newsletter and showed me a copy, I became very interested. I'm a piano teacher but I also love to write, so I cautiously asked, "Can I have a corner and write each month in your newsletters?" She smiled and said, "Sure, but take a whole column." That's how Joy's Corner began!

I guess I was bold in asking, but I have never regretted it because writing those articles turned out to be a great blessing for me. After about nine years, I realized those articles could become a book. *Peace in Prison* was the result. And another nine years has come and gone, and now *Jesus in Jail* is the result.

There is another chapter in my life that strongly influenced my feelings about those who are in prison. It happened when I was nine years of age. My grandfather was sent to the penitentiary just north of San Francisco for two years. As a child, I fully remember the sting of the neighbor's gossip.

So, in writing "Joy's Corner" (and also, later, "Peace in Prison,") I liked to think of words of encouragement that would be special for those behind bars. And writing "Joy's Corner" has given me a lot to think about.

And now, *Jesus in Jail* is a second book that has been written and organized, based on "Joy's Corner."

God bless you, wherever you are—no matter your circumstances, God really is there for YOU.

God's richest blessings to you as you experience *Jesus in Jail.*

My love and good thoughts to you, dear reader.

Sincerely yours,

Joy Dutton-Seltzer

Exceeding Great Reward

One hot day in New Mexico, I was traveling back home from visiting a good friend. As I left her home, she went on to work, and so there was no time for my usual morning worship.

As I drove along Elephant Butte Dam, near Truth or Consequences, New Mexico, I prayed for a nice place to park, asking God for a "spot with a view." Soon, I came upon a view that nearly took my breath away.

The beauty of the butte, the pristine blue of the water in the dam, the fluffy white clouds, and a shady tree answered my prayer perfectly. I parked, got out, and walked around a bit. No other human was there. But God was, and I knew it.

As it was very hot even at 10 a.m., I got back in the car and turned on the air conditioning. Then, I put my Bible on the steering wheel to read it and have a good worship.

My next prayer was this: *Lord, this is such a beautiful spot on earth, please give me a special Bible text—one that is all my own. Words from You that I will never forget.* And He did just that— for ME!

In Genesis, the very first book of the Bible, in chapter 15, the first verse, it says, "… the word of the Lord came unto Abram in a vision…." (Abram was later called Abraham.) And He said to him, "Fear not, Abram: I am thy shield, and thy exceeding great reward."

I read again, "…Thy exceeding great reward." Then I nearly shouted: "…Thy EXCEEDING GREAT reward."

When I was a small child in church school, studying about how Jesus loves me, there were many times when I knew for sure that God was intervening in my life; I knew God was there.

But now this "exceeding great reward." WOW!!! I don't have to wait for heaven to have my "reward." Just like Abram in his vision, I can have God PRESENT in my life all the time—ALL DAY, ALL NIGHT! Now, God is my special Companion all the time, no matter what the circumstances are.

> *Now, God is my special Companion all the time, no matter what the circumstances are.*

I don't think I prayed after reading that God was my exceeding great reward; I just talked to Him. His Word, written out by Moses centuries ago, became personal to ME on that day, and I shall never forget it.

Now, God is my special Companion all the time. The Father, our Savior, and the Holy Spirit are present in my life, giving me peace and joy—no matter what the circumstances of the day are.

Abram, myself—, and YOU—we all have that same promise. HEAVEN is not our reward, GOD is!

Every human being sees God differently, and God sees and loves each of us in His own special way. He loves us just as we are.

And we can have Him right now and always if we want Him. He's not looking for our flaws. He is envisioning our possibilities. No matter where we are, God Himself IS our REWARD.

The Ultimate Look of Love

Looking at my fourth-grade picture, I see two lonely eyes. I remember thinking, "Will I ever have any friends?"

My dad worked at night and slept in the daytime. He worked thirteen nights and then had one Sunday free for his family. On our family days, we usually went to the beach. San Diego, California, has great beach weather. So my brother and I got to see Dad about two days every month.

I loved that man. And I knew he loved me. We didn't talk about love. We just knew it was there.

On my sixty-fourth birthday, years later, I drove my dad to a favorite restaurant for my birthday. Dad was eighty-eight years old by now. When we got home, he started to get out of the car, then returned, and sat down. He looked full in my face and said, "I have loved you ever since the day you were born." My response was, "Oh, Dad, I always knew it." I saw the look of love.

Why were those words so important to me? Well, the men in our family just didn't say, "I love you." It seems the words got stuck in their throats! Yet they were all loving and kind men.

So, I knew I was loved by Dad. But seeing him so seldom as a child, his love was not enough. I was lonely for the look of love.

This loneliness followed me for years. My brother had his dog, Happy. After school each afternoon, my brother and Happy talked to each other on the back doorstep. And, to be honest, throughout all his life, Happy may have been his only true love. Dogs can sometimes be closer to a person than any human.

I have just finished reading *Buddy* by M. H. Herlong. The book is about the incredible love of a boy for his dog. They saw and gave their love to each other in that special way we all yearn for love. Our need to love and BE loved is so intense, we must have a relative, friend, or at least a pet to fill that hole in our heart.

As I was thinking about this most basic need early this morning, I realized I'm always looking for a deep friendship—for that look of love. Yet, too many times I have looked past the deepest friendship one could have. The presence of God is the only true and constant fulfillment that can satisfy our need for love.

A guilt trip is too often the cause of ignoring the ultimate Love of our lives. The disciple Peter denied Jesus Christ at His trial, just before He was nailed to the cross. Luke 22:54–62 tells the story of Peter's terrible sin and the ultimate look of love from Jesus.

And any crime, any sin that any of us commits, is just like Peter's denial. Yet, when that cock crowed, Jesus turned and looked full into the face of Peter. Their eyes locked. At that moment, Peter realized what he had just done (Luke 22:61) because Jesus had predicted his denial (Luke 22:34).

The look of love from Jesus to Peter turned his life around. That fisherman by trade became a "fisher of men," telling others about Jesus's love by dying on the cross, His resurrection, and His promise of a home in heaven in the future. What wondrous love!

> *The presence of God is the only true and constant fulfillment that can satisfy our need for love.*

The presence of God is the only true and constant fulfillment that can satisfy our need for love. Just for the asking, we may have this most awesome Friendship. You may be saying, "But I'm too evil for God. You don't know my crimes. Could God actually want Me?" Yes! Yes! Yes!

No matter how great the crime or sin, that look of love is available for you right now—just look up and ask!

In 1 John 3:20, we are told, "For if our heart condemn us, God is greater than our heart…." What a relief! God knows us completely, even our thoughts. Yet He loves us; He wants to enter our hearts and give us the true life we have always wanted.

The cross of Jesus is love in its purest form. Jesus's Spirit in your heart is the deepest love you can ever have. Let God into your heart. Let true love make you into your very best self.

Then 1 John 1:9 gives us this assurance: "If we confess our sins, he is faithful and just to forgive us our sins, and to cleanse us from all unrighteousness." Now THAT is ultimate, everlasting love!

God's Incredible Plan

God's incredible plan and His purpose for your life are the same thing.

Creation, the cross, and Jesus's second coming are the three big events that connect you and me to God's eternal plan and His purpose. He has a plan for this world—for today and every day. This plan is as huge as the universe and as tiny as each atom that makes you who you are. Every part of you was planned and designed by God.

Unfortunately, evil showed its ugly head long ago through the very first people God created. The Bible is the book that tells how sin destroyed our original face-to-face connection with our Creator (Gen. 3:1–10). The Bible is the book that tells us of His incredible plan to save us FROM our sins. The Bible is a book about God's saving love.

God's PLAN or PURPOSE was to create a world and make it beautiful: light, air, trees, flowers, sun, moon, stars, fish, birds, and animals. Then the highest of God's creation: PEOPLE—Adam and Eve.

The joy of Adam, Eve, and their Creator was God's very desire. In the garden, walking together, they talked about the pure love they had for each other. It was all good. Caressing a bird, petting a lion, holding a butterfly, walking on carpets of vibrant green grass, eating ripe fruit right off the trees, hearing angels' songs, smelling the aromas of heaven—these were all beautiful and unspoiled delights without end (Gen. 1:26–31, Gen. 2:1–25).

But one day, the enemy of God did his dirty tricks, and the world has been in a tragic situation ever since then (Gen. 3:1–3).

When we question, "WHY?" No matter the tragedy, we can rightfully look back to the tree of decision, also called "the tree of good and evil." The devil spoke through a snake, and Eve was deceived. She reached out, took, and ate the forbidden fruit. Adam also fell for the lie Satan expressed: "Ye shall not surely die" (Gen. 3:4).

Yet, the tragedy of sin came with a PROMISE. The promise was the plan of salvation (Gen. 3:15). This was GOD'S INCREDIBLE PLAN!

In the Holy Bible, the first two chapters in the book of Genesis and last two chapters in the book of Revelation give us a picture of beauty and purity—without sin. The entire rest of the Bible describes how God, in His incredible love, dealt with the problem of sin.

I think of Cain, offering a sacrifice of fruits and vegetables instead of a lamb (Gen. 4:3). Cain knew this was a sin and that his offering was not acceptable to God. Why? Because the blood of the lamb pointed forward to Jesus as the Lamb who would be killed to take away our sins. But Cain rebelled and refused to offer a lamb, insisting that his fruits and vegetables were equally as good. This kind of wickedness grew year by year until, in the sixth chapter of Genesis, God had to do something about the cumulative evil that the people continually chose (Gen. 6:5–6).

However, there were always a few people who chose God over evil. Noah was willing to do God's will. The Lord gave him blueprints for a large boat, an ark. Noah spent 120 years building the ark and preaching—warning people about a coming flood (Gen. 6:7–22; Gen. 7:1–24; Gen. 8:1–19). Noah and his family alone chose God's will.

After the flood, the Lord started things up again. Noah and his family, along with the animals that had been protected from the flood, left the ark, as new vegetation began to grow. By and by, the earth became populated again. But there was a repeat of the tragedy of people turning to evil. Now, as they built the tower of Babel (in an attempt to reach heaven to never again be hurt by a flood), their evil grew to such desperate proportions that God had to intervene again (Gen. 11:4–8).

Sin, the devil's specialty, became so normal for people, that God had to pluck out another person for His plan and purpose.

Abraham, a man of God's choosing, became "a father of many nations" (Gen. 17:4). Abraham was 100 years old and his wife, Sarah, was 90 when the promised son, Isaac, was born. In Genesis 22:1–18, we find an incredible story of how Abraham took Isaac (who symbolized Jesus as God's Only Son) and was willing to sacrifice Isaac as an offering to the Lord. Isaac's willingness to allow Abraham to sacrifice him also came from a heart that trusted God. God honored these two, as He blessed them with a special promise.

Isaac had only two children, twin boys, Jacob and Esau. Jacob gave birth to 12 sons who later were called the "tribe of Israel." These children of Jacob were also called "God's chosen" (Ps. 105:6). Esau, the other son of Isaac, was much like Cain. He hated Jacob and was not interested in the privileges God had given him. Later in history, the Bible records the blood battles between God's chosen people of Israel and the Edomites, who were Esau's descendants.

Why would twin brothers turn against each other? Because Esau carelessly gave away his God-given birthright as the firstborn son for a pot of lentil stew (Gen. 25:32–33). His brother, Jacob, had different priorities; he had a wrestling match with the Angel of the Lord, and he persevered until the Angel blessed him and changed his name to Israel (Gen. 32:24–28). Evil and good were shown in contrast to each other once more. As history moved on, it is interesting to note that when Israel chose to let the Lord lead in battle, Israel won the victory.

There is more—much more—continuing in the next chapter....

More of God's Incredible Plan

The ten plagues of Egypt (Exod. 7:17 through 12:31), leading to the deliverance of Israel from Egypt and through the Red Sea, was certainly a great miracle. Not one of God's people died.

Yet, just three days after this great miracle of deliverance, God's children murmured their complaints against God—as they did for the next forty years of their journey to the promised land.

Indeed, God has unique ways to fight a battle! This was not the last time that God intervened for His people in a miraculous way. The book of Joshua (Josh. 6:2–20) describes Joshua's battle of Jericho as "...the wall fell down flat...." I'm always amazed at how God's battles are so different than when the people fought without asking for God's blessings first. And waiting for the Lord.

Many people have said to me: The Old Testament is full of battles. I can't serve a God like that." But I ask, "Look at the different types of battles. When they did not ask for God's help, the battles were terrible. Yet, when they asked for God's help, the battles resulted in a victory without a bloody mess.

And yet, shortly after Jericho, the Israelites struck out on a battle all their own. They did not consult God first. Thirty-six men lost their lives because of ignoring God and not putting Him first—before the battle.

Israel had to flee in disgrace and run for their lives. They learned a big lesson: that they should ask for God's guidance before acting. They were learning to TRUST God.

God's incredible strategy for battle is mentioned many times, as seen in the following examples.

- At Jericho, a spectacular battle was won. Singing and blowing horns (not fighting) brought those walls down.

- After that spectacular battle, only some of the Israelites decided—without asking God—to capture a tiny town: Ai. Thirty men lost their lives. The others ran in disgrace for their lives, entirely defeated.

  The enemies were all dead—and the choir sang God's praises! God's incredible strategy includes helping us fight our personal battles, too. It is God's fight, and our part is to have FAITH in His ability to help us.

  The next time they tried to capture Ai, they talked to God first. They had learned to trust God—to ask His will first, then act. To me, as I face my tiny personal battles, I know God wants to be acknowledged. Then, trusting God's impressions on my mind, things turn out best. The enemies were all dead—and the choir sang God's praises! God's incredible strategy includes helping us fight our personal battles, too. It is God's fight, and our part is to have FAITH in His ability to help us.

Another example of God's miraculous care for His people is given in 2 Chron. 20:1–24, when Jehoshaphat prayed, fasted, and sent the choir first into battle while Ammonites, Moabites, and the inhabitants of Mount Seir came with war on their minds. However, when the people of the Lord marched toward those enemies, they were amazed to find that the three armies had killed each other! The enemies were all dead—and the choir sang God's praises! God had rescued His people without a struggle!

When Elijah, the prophet of God, was on Mt. Carmel, facing the false prophets of Baal, all the people of Israel finally bowed down and admitted, "the Lord, He is God" (1 Kings 18:17–39).

When the Syrian army tried to capture the prophet Elisha, the soldiers were smitten with blindness (2 Kings 6:8–18). God's assurance in any battle is sure: it is part of God's way of dealing with the enemies of God's people. You don't need to fight the battle! Just stand still and see the salvation of the Lord on your behalf (2 Chron. 20:17).

David faced the giant Goliath with these words: "...I come to thee in the name of the Lord..." (1 Sam. 17:45). God's incredible plan includes helping us fight our personal battles, too.

In my own personal battles, I like to think of God's assurance to me: "...be not afraid...for the battle is not yours, but God's" (2 Chron. 20:15).

The Bible verse 1 Timothy 6:12 affirms: "Fight the good fight of FAITH..." (emphasis added). It is God's fight, and our part is to have FAITH in His ability to help us.

Again, 1 John 5:4 assures us: "...this is the victory that overcometh the world, even our FAITH" (emphasis added).

Ephesians 6:14–17 lists the armor we need to wear while fighting life's battles. It includes the following: the BELT of truth, the BREASTPLATE of Christ's righteousness, the SHOES of the gospel of peace, the SHIELD of faith, the HELMET of salvation, and the SWORD, which is the word of God.

There finally had to be a solution for SIN. All sin is abominable to God. Jesus Christ, our Savior, came to earth to be born just as we are, to give an example of right-living (righteousness), and finally die on the cross for ALL sin.

HE WAS GOD'S INCREDIBLE PLAN in action. Salvation for us all (if we choose Him).

Most of us have read or have heard the creation story: the beginning of the plan. This is written in Genesis, the first book of the Bible. How could any of us miss the story of the cross, as described in Matthew 27:27–54, Mark 15:22–37, Luke 23:18–44, John 19:16–30)? The next part of the plan is in the very near future.

What is that plan? This same Jesus who was killed on the cross, who rose back to life three days later, and who returned to His home in heaven—HE IS COMING BACK! This is the best part of His plan. No more sin—ever again. You have a heaven to win. A hell to shun.

Indeed, the best part of His plan is His death on the cross for our sin. He died to save us from our sins and forgive us our sins so we can be with Him in heaven SOON—VERY SOON. GOD HAS A GREAT PLAN FOR YOUR FUTURE!

God's Incredible Love

God is not sorry He made you. He has plans for you. Silently, tell Him your story. He can read your mind. Remember, God created your brain.

The crush of noise, the silence of solitude, the pain of your body or emotions, even honest guilt, is prison enough. In some ways, we all have a touch of prison-life. The truth is that God specializes in being close to people in jail.

No matter WHERE you are or what you have done, God really does have plans for you. "For I know the plans I have for you," declares the Lord, "plans to prosper you and not to harm you, plans to give you hope and a future" (Jer. 29:11, NIV).

Jesus stands at the door of your heart just waiting to hear you say, "Come in. You are welcome in my heart." JOY and PEACE walk in with Him. They accompany the presence of the Lord—no matter where you are, even if you are in prison. Jesus is GOD'S INCREDIBLE LOVE. John 3:16 (NIV) says, "For God so loved the world that he gave his one and only Son, that whoever believes in him shall not perish but have eternal life." Whoever means YOU.

Eugene Peterson's The Message puts it this way: "This is how much God loved the world: He gave his Son, his one and only Son. And this is why: so that no one need be destroyed; by believing in him, anyone can have a whole and lasting life" (John 3:16, TM).

John 3:17 (TM) goes on to assure us: "God didn't go to all the trouble of sending his Son merely to point an accusing finger, telling the world how bad it was. He came to help, to put the world right again."

But, you may be wondering, "what about my crimes—and my sins? Well, just let Him into your heart. Tell him your story. He knows how to

forgive. Actually He did that already at the cross. In 1 John 1:9, His promise is this: "If we confess our sins, he is faithful and just to forgive us our
sins, and to cleanse us from all unrighteousness."

Jesus is ALWAYS at the door of your heart, waiting to come in. He
assures us: "...lo, I am with you always, even unto the end of the world.
Amen" (Matt. 28:20).

In time, JOY will shine on your face; PEACE will grow in your heart.
You really can live in His plan of LOVE right where you are, right now.

The Lion's Roar

It has been observed in the wild that a lion can fool his "next meal" into coming closer to him with a "Squeak, squeak, squeak," and then terrorize the victim with a ROAR that paralyzes him.

The power of that roar ensures the lion of his lunch. It's a trick of the wild. Someone else knows that trick. Satan. He's full of tricks. He knows the power he has over us, as we are drawn to his attractions, whatever they may be.

Without the POWER OF THE HOLY SPIRIT, we humans have no defense when the lion roars. The power of the devil's roar is too much for us. But he's no match for our Savior who conquered "that roar" on the cross.

Now, 1 Peter 5:8 says, "Be sober, be vigilant; because your adversary the devil, as a roaring lion, walketh about, seeking whom he may devour." Peter knew what he was talking about.

In the Garden of Gethsemane, the Lord had asked Peter, James, and John to pray, while He went a little way off and prayed on His own. Too sleepy to even pray, Peter and the others slept, while their Savior agonized alone over His own destiny.

The next morning, Jesus was on trial before Herod, and Peter, not protected by prayer, denied his Lord three times. Yes, Peter knew by experience what it was to be devoured by the devil.

Daniel, a prophet of the Old Testament, prayed three times a day (Dan. 6:10), even in defiance of the officers of the court. They convinced King Darius to make a law to kill anyone who prayed to any "god" other than the king.

After catching Daniel praying at his window, the king had no choice but to throw Daniel into the lion's den. Prepared by prayer, Daniel was safe from these hungry animals.

The next morning, very early, the king, himself came to see if Daniel's God could protect him. With gladness, the king had Daniel lifted out of the den, and instead tossed the court officials into the den. The lions had those men for breakfast. The lions were hungry, but God, Himself protected His trusting prophet (Dan. 6:24).

From a squeak— "this can't be all that bad"—to a ROAR—"Now, you've done it," prayer for the power of the Holy Spirit is our only protection.

There's Power in Loneliness

School was a challenge for me because I was made to start school too soon. I was a late bloomer. Later, the trauma of high school, of trying and sometimes even failing, drove me into a loneliness that took years and years to recover from.

As an adult, I was in a lonely state of existing. I already was a piano teacher (and I thank God I had my students to love and that I was loved by them), but then I began to write. I became fascinated with words. In those days, I simply filled up pages of "feelings." But I just didn't want anyone to know how I felt, so I burned up all my writing.

I put on a good front for others. Why should I bring down their emotions, just because mine were in the pits?

After a bit, I started writing seriously and saving what I wrote in my top drawer. In time, I needed a second drawer. Now I have six drawers of notes. Occasionally, I would look through them, laugh at some, toss some, and then realize—because of the SOLITUDE in my life—I was becoming a writer as well as a piano teacher.

It is my desire, dear reader, that YOU, too, can look beyond your present circumstances and write YOUR story. Think about "what went wrong," and how to change it. How to get beyond the deep gut hurt and reach for something beyond yourself, to make a different future for yourself…and also think about someone else for a change.

These texts have done wonders for me at difficult times:

Genesis 16:13 "…Thou God seest me…"

Deuteronomy 4:31 (NIV) "For the Lord your God is a merciful God; he will not abandon or destroy you…."

Psalm 68:6 "God setteth the solitary in families: he bringeth out those which are bound with chains...."

Psalm 121:5 (NIV) "The Lord watches over you...."

Isaiah 49:16 "Behold, I have graven thee upon the palms of my hands...."

Jeremiah 31:3 (NIV) "I have loved you with an everlasting love...."

God bless you, wherever you are—no matter your circumstances, God really is there for YOU.

Power in Peace

Why do we struggle so with anxiety or anger when we don't get our way? All of us experience these emotions. And perhaps they serve us well for a while. But there comes a time when our whole inner core wants relief.

> *It is important to communicate with the ONE PERSON who can give you true peace. That PERSON is God.*

"Peace at any cost" is not true peace. When we stand for the right, there is a certain peace from within—a peace that goes beyond human understanding. It is important to communicate with the ONE PERSON who can give you true peace. That PERSON is God.

PEACE. How do you arrive at peace's door? Open the door of your heart to the Lord, and experience it especially where you are right now. King David found this peace early on in his life. His psalm reassures us: "I will both lay me down in peace, and sleep: for thou, Lord, only makest me dwell in safety" (Ps. 4:8.).

Forgiveness is ready just for the asking. Jesus said, "...ask, and ye shall receive, that your joy may be full" (John 16:24). This is not an empty promise. He forgives as soon as you ask for forgiveness for your wrong—for your sins—for ALL the things you have done or said that could displease God in any way. PEACE results from forgiveness.

It is important to communicate with the ONE PERSON who can give you true peace. That PERSON is God, Himself. He's always ready to hear your confession. Prayer is NOT difficult. No one has to talk to another human to get this peace. God is ready to hear you—right NOW.

Prayer is the one form of communication that can take place in your mind. God knows exactly what you are thinking. Wake up praying. Go to sleep praying. Sincere personal prayer is always answered.

There is a power in PEACE that creates personal freedom—no matter where we are or what we're doing. May God bless you with this peace right now.

Prayer Power

Prayer has POWER. When I pray, asking for something, I have a God (so do you!) who answers prayer. He answers: YES, YES, YES. He's eager to answer our prayers.

The first "yes" is often immediate, always on course, and always just what you need. The second "yes" is "Yes, but wait." And the third "yes" is "Yes, but my solution is even better."

We have a God we can trust. God does answer prayers. There is POWER IN PRAYER.

I fell asleep while driving on a trip in New Mexico. The road was so straight, and I was sleepy—not a good combination. As the tires rolled over the road bumps on the left side of the road, I jerked awake, and screamed, "HELP!"

Fortunately, no other car was on the road at the moment, and the road bumps woke me up. I looked both ways with relief and smoothly drove onto the right side of the highway, shaking, and very grateful. That one-word prayer "HELP" was answered as soon as I prayed it. Awesome God!

Sometimes, God asks us to wait. In the second grade in our little church school, Miss B. taught us about the cross of Jesus and what it meant. I understood her, and I wanted Jesus to be MY Savior. With Jesus in my heart, I began to pray for others. From that day until I was seventeen years old, I prayed for my dad.

I loved Dad; he was a very good man, but he wasn't going to church. I prayed for him every day for eleven years before he was finally baptized. That was the happiest day of my life. God answered my prayer for Dad. WAIT...sometimes our prayers take a while. God KNOWS your prayer. He is in process. Don't give up. God's time is always best.

I'm a piano player, and I also teach piano lessons. In fact, teaching has been my life's work. Because my fingers are very short, one teacher told me I'd never be a piano player, and this was just after I had played the very difficult Flight of the Bumble Bee by Rimsky-Korsakov.

Yes, I knew I would never be able to play Malagueña because that piano piece is full of octaves, and, indeed, my fingers never grew long enough to play magnificent songs such as that. And you must believe I prayed for my fingers to grow longer, as I really wanted to play everything on the keyboard. I love playing what I CAN play, but there is so much more I could play if my fingers were just a little longer. I prayed for longer fingers for many years. Finally when I reached my thirtieth birthday, I looked at my hands and accepted my short fingers, realizing that God answered my prayers in another way. I needed to learn gratitude for the fingers I already had. Now I play very well, having learned a few tricks to work around the "octave" problem; I play with delight...as I teach...as I play in concerts...and as I play for the church, for my family, and, many times, just for myself.

When I think about my limitations on the piano, I realize that God is just keeping me humble while I perform. God is all-wise. HE always knows best.

His "Yes, NOW," or "Yes, but wait," or His "Yes, but I have a better plan" is sufficient. So is His GRACE.

God's Word Is Powerful

"LET THERE BE LIGHT: and there was light" (Gen. 1:3) (emphasis added). The Bible tells of the beginnings of this old world. There is power in God's Word. He spoke and the world was created in just six days.

"PEACE, BE STILL" (Mark 4:39) (emphasis added). In the middle of a storm on the lake, Jesus spoke these famous words. The boat was sinking, but, as He spoke these three little words, immediately, the storm was over. The wind died down, and the rain stopped; the lake became calm and quiet. The storm passed with the sound of Jesus's powerful words: "Peace, be still."

"Father, FORGIVE THEM; for they know not what they do…" (Luke 23:34) (emphasis added). These powerful words of Jesus were spoken while He hung on the cross; His words were meant for the very persons who nailed Him there.

"FOR GOD SO LOVED THE WORLD, that he gave his only begotten Son, that whosoever believeth in him should not perish, but have everlasting life" (John 3:16) (emphasis added). These words were from Jesus's lips as He was talking to Nicodemus in a discussion the two men had one night. These are saving words for the eternal salvation of millions of people—and for you personally, too! Looking to Jesus, we all can have confidence that Jesus's WORDS are true.

"Thy word have I hid in my heart, that I might not sin against thee" (Ps. 119:11). God's WORD is powerful, even preventing us from sinning as we listen to His Word.

"…Son, THY SINS BE FORGIVEN THEE" (Mark 2:5) (emphasis added). That was Jesus talking to the paralytic who was let down from the roof to lie before Him. This man was in agony over his sin. Jesus, thought-fully spoke forgiveness for his sin first, and then He healed his body.

"Heaviness in the heart of man maketh it stoop: but a good word maketh it glad" (Prov. 12:25). King Solomon, the wisest man on earth, wrote this verse because he realized how important a "good word" is.

Look how descriptively King Solomon writes. "A word fitly spoken is like apples of gold in pictures of silver" (Prov. 25:11). How often someone has said an encouraging word to me, and my day brightened immediately. I really try to give the favor back to others by encouraging others with just a word. Here and there, a little word can make the difference.

Matthew 24:35 tells us: "Heaven and earth shall pass away, but my words shall not pass away." What a wonderful promise from Jesus!

James, the half-brother of Jesus, wrote a great book in the Bible. It's just five chapters long, but you can see the influence that Jesus had on his character and, ultimately, on his thinking. This ideal is high, but worth reaching for. "...If any man offend not in word, the same is a perfect man..." (James 3:2).

There is a lot more to the power of God's words. Look at Colossians 3:16: "Let the word of Christ dwell in you richly in all wisdom; teaching and admonishing one another in psalms and hymns and spiritual songs, singing with grace in your hearts to the Lord."

In Jesus's prayer for His disciples—and indeed for the whole world, (for us!)—just before Gethsemane and Calvary, John 17:17 says, "Sanctify them through thy truth: thy word is truth." We can absolutely count on the words of God, Jesus, and Their Book, the Holy Bible.

"IN THE BEGINNING was the Word, and the Word was with God, and the Word was God" (John 1:1) (emphasis added). This declares that Jesus is the Word.

In the story of the man who had a spirit of an unclean devil, Jesus rebuked the devil, saying, "...hold thy peace, and come out of him....And they were all amazed, and spake among themselves, saying, What a word is this! for with authority and power he commandeth the unclean spirits, and they come out" (Luke 4:35–36). Jesus was always amazing people with the power of His WORDS.

At the very end of the Bible, John, the revelator, was describing heaven. In Revelation 21, the description is in powerful picture words: "...and there shall be NO MORE DEATH, neither SORROW, nor CRY-ING, neither shall there be any more PAIN: for the former things are passed away" (Rev. 21:4) (emphasis added). What wonderful words of promise! Words that we can believe!

The God Who Sees

It all started when Sarai, Abram's wife suggested a way to help God do His job. You see, Abram and Sarai were very old. Yet God made a promise that they would have a baby. This promised child would be an ancestor of the promised Messiah.

Years swiftly passed, yet no child; then Sarai had an idea. She told Abram to "...go in unto my maid; it may be that I may obtain children by her" (Gen. 16:2).

As Adam fell for Eve's mistake, so Abram listened to his wife, Sarai. So he went in to Hagar, "...and she conceived" (Gen. 16:4).

Then strange things began to happen. At first, it looks like a family fight. After Hagar conceived, she then turned against Sarai. Hagar despised Sarai. When Sarai pled for help from Abram, he advised, "...Behold, thy maid is in thine hand; do to her as it pleaseth thee" (Gen. 16:6).

Talk about a low point in life! When Sarai dealt harshly with her, Hagar fled from Sarai's presence; she simply ran away.

"The angel of the Lord found her by a fountain of water in the wilderness...." Of course, Hagar felt that she was all alone. Yet, now the Angel spoke to her: "...Hagar, Sarai's maid, whence camest thou? and whither wilt thou go?" (Gen. 16:7–8).

Hagar admitted the truth. "I flee from the face of my mistress Sarai. And the angel of the Lord said unto her, Return to thy mistress....I will multiply thy seed exceedingly, that it shall not be numbered for multitude" (Gen. 16:8–10). And it happened just that way.

The Angel of the Lord asked Hagar to do a very humiliating and difficult thing. He told her to go back to Sarai and submit herself to her.

Dear reader, pause and absorb her feelings just now. Oh yes, she did have a choice. She could have continued running away, but thirst and possible starvation would have been her lot. She could have sat by that well in the desert and not moved anywhere, too depressed to leave that spot. But she ultimately made the best choice.

After the Angel of the Lord spoke, she exclaimed, "Thou God seest me…" (Gen. 16:13). What a privilege she had, what an honor. She named the well Beer lahai roi, which means "You are the God who sees" (Gen. 16:13, NIV).

Often, when I'm in a tough spot and things are going terribly for me, I think of Hagar. When she realized, "Thou God seest me…," she gained strength to return to Sarai's tent and in time her son, Ishmael, was born.

Abram and Sarai had their own trials of waiting and wondering when the promised child would be born. It was a long time to wait. Sarai was 90 years old and Abram was 100 years old. While they waited, God gave Abram the new name of Abraham and Sarai the new name of Sarah and promised again that they would have a son. Then Isaac, the promised son, was finally born. Isaac, their son's name, means laughter. After all that waiting, they had good reason to laugh and be happy. They could all say, THOU GOD SEEST ME.

Many years later, the prophet Jeremiah assured us that God indeed does have a plan for each of us. I hope you memorize this little jewel: "For I know the plans I have for you," declares the Lord, "plans to prosper you and not harm you, plans to give you hope and a future" (Jer. 29:11, NIV).

Please remember that God has a thousand ways to make the best turn out of ANY circumstance.

It Was the Worst Night

Jacob was walking in the dark—all alone. Suddenly someone started wrestling with him. He wrestled back. He was a very strong man, but he could not win this battle. He fought for his life. Hour after hour, he struggled, using every muscle he had. It was the worse night of his life (Gen. 32:24).

But first, let's go back a bit. Jacob's grandfather was the great man Abraham, who was chosen by God as the father of His nation, Israel. Through some very remarkable situations, a Redeemer was promised to Abraham and his children for generations to come. Matthew, chapter one, tells of all these generations from Abraham to Jesus Christ Immanuel, the Savior of the world.

But here was Jacob—many years before the Savior was even born in Bethlehem—and he was struggling for his life. He knew about the Promise. But he was not thinking about it then. Hour after dark hour, the wrestling continued. Frightened, alone, and feeling guilty, he just kept on struggling until dawn.

Genesis 32:24 spells out the story this way: "And Jacob was left alone; and there wrestled a man with him until the breaking of the day." Whew! What a night, the very worst for Jacob. Then, oh, how I love that word: "THEN." Verse 25 opens up the mystery of WHO the wrestler was. It reveals: "And when he saw that he prevailed not against him, he touched the hollow of his thigh; and the hollow of Jacob's thigh was out of joint, as he wrestled with him." Ouch, a bad night, indeed.

Jacob was not only exhausted, now he was LAME. A very bad night for certain.

Then the man said, "Let me go, for the day breaketh" (Gen. 32:26, first part). Instantly, Jacob recognized who he was struggling with—the Lord Himself. And Jacob quickly answered, "I will not let thee go, except thou bless me" (Gen. 32:26, last part). Jacob then acknowledged who the "man" was. In verse 30, Jacob admits, "...for I have seen God face to face, and my life is preserved."

We all have struggles in the darkest hours of our lives, but the dawn of a new day gives hope for a better life. Each day gives us the chance to choose the God who wrestles with us in the dark.

Jacob finally realized it was the BEST night of his life—wrestling with God.

A Masterpiece

"Live one day at a time and make each day a masterpiece." This is what a friend said to me a long time ago.

All afternoon we had been sharing our miseries, yet she gave me a gorgeous smile as she was leaving. I asked, "With all your troubles, you can still smile—how come?" That's when she said, "And make each day a masterpiece."

Psalm 105:18 tells a story of a very brave man who chose to make each day a masterpiece. The Message Bible tells us, "They put cruel chains on his ankles, an iron collar around his neck...." He was treated as a dangerous criminal. And yet he was innocent. That man was Joseph, son of Jacob and grandson of Isaac, who was Abraham's son.

Genesis, chapters 37 and 39, tell of Joseph's adventures: a coat of many colors, eleven brothers, a pit, a slave for ten years, and innocent but thrown in prison. The next thing he knew, Joseph was in shackles in the darkness of the dungeon, yet he had peace as he trusted his life to God.

During all of those trials, whenever Joseph was tempted, his first thought was of God. "...how then can I do this great wickedness, and sin against God?" (Gen. 39:9). Even though he was a slave in a foreign country, he was aware of the presence of God. Joseph suffered for his integrity.

"Joseph gradually gained the confidence of the keeper of the prison, and was finally entrusted with the charge of all the prisoners. It was the part he acted in the prison—the integrity of his daily life and his sympathy for those who were in trouble and distress—that opened the way for his future prosperity and honor."1

Indeed, with God, Joseph found a way to make each day a masterpiece. After three years in prison, he interpreted Pharaoh's dreams, became the highest officer just under Pharaoh, and saved the country of Egypt during a seven-year famine. Through the ordeal of the famine, Joseph's family soon moved from Israel to Egypt to live, and they were reunited there with Joseph. A family of 70 became a nation of millions. Long after Joseph died, Moses led that nation of Israel back to their Promised Land.

Punished for Praying

When Darius, the Mede, took the throne from the Babylonians, he made Daniel the first president over two other presidents. All three of them were to preside over the large kingdom of 120 governors. Daniel's excellent spirit caused the king to prefer him above all the other rulers, and set him over the entire kingdom (Dan. 6:1–3).

There is something special about a person who is inside God's will. Daniel lived so close to the Lord that his character was without flaw. Daniel had always complied with the king's commands, but, this time, his allegiance was to the King of kings. This high position caused jealousy among the other leaders in this new kingdom. Not being satisfied with their new leadership positions, they looked for a way to get Daniel's position.

> *There is something special about a person who is inside God's will. Daniel lived so close to the Lord that his character was without flaw. Daniel had always complied with the king's commands, but, this time, his allegiance was to the King of kings.*

However, Daniel was a man who was true to his Creator. They tried to trap him in a mistake—a flaw of some sort. But Daniel lived so close to his Lord, that he was not making mistakes. His character was without a flaw. They could find no error or fault in him. He was blameless.

Actually, Daniel had a reputation of being a "pray-er." While he was a servant of the previous king, Nebuchadnezzar, Daniel prayed before interpreting the king's dreams. (This story is in Daniel chapters 2 and 4.)

Later, during the banquet for the next king, Daniel interpreted the handwriting on the wall that said, "...Mene, Mene, Tekel, Upharsin" (Dan. 5:25). This was a message written by God's own hand on the wall of the palace. Daniel informed King Belshazzar that his kingdom would transfer to the Medes and the Persians that very night.

Now Daniel, whose habit was turning to the Lord, was lifted up to a very high position in the kingdom. He was now the first president over the new kingdom of the Medes.

Soon the other presidents observed his praying habits. The secret of his character was his prayer life. The two other presidents and the princes looked up at the window of his home. Morning, noon, and evening he knelt down by the open window and poured out his heart to God.

There is something special about a person who is inside God's will. You can count on their character to ring true. Daniel was no exception to this trait of holiness. He heard about the trickery of the others but he proceeded to continue his habit of prayer. With the window open, and his eyes lifted heavenward, he continued voicing his earnest prayers.

Meanwhile the others, seething with jealousy, devised a scheme. They met with the king and told him a lie. They said, "All the presidents of the kingdom, the governors, and the princes, the counsellors, and the captains, have consulted together to establish a royal statute..." (Dan. 6:7). (Actually, Daniel and some others were NOT there at that meeting.)

They continued to lay out their devious plan: "... to make a firm decree, that whosoever shall ask a petition of any God or man for thirty days, save of thee, O king, he shall be cast into the den of lions" (Dan. 6:7).

"Now, O king, establish the decree, and sign the writing, that it be not changed, according to the law of the Medes and Persians, which altereth not" (Dan. 6:8).

Ignorant of their devious plan and feeling somewhat flattered, the king signed the decree. Soon, he regretted signing.

The enemies of Daniel became spies, seeking to trap him as he prayed. Wisely, Daniel continued praying as before—three times each day. Daniel chose to keep his window open, so it was easy for the spies to catch Daniel praying.

Just like children, the enemies of Daniel ran to the king and tattled on him. Daniel had always complied with the king's commands, but, this time, his allegiance was to the King of kings.

King Darius had no choice but to cast Daniel down into the den of lions. Daniel trusted his God. He had no fear. But the king was in misery all night.

Early the next morning, the king came to the den. He shouted down to Daniel. Daniel responded, "My God hath sent his angel, and hath shut the lions' mouths…" (Dan. 6:22). Just think how God honored the faithful prayers of Daniel!

"Daniel stands before the world today as a worthy example of Christian fearlessness and fidelity."2

Yes, Daniel was "punished for praying," but God had a better plan and saved him right there with the lions.

In the Mud

Jeremiah, an Old Testament prophet, was bold and truthful when God gave him a prophecy for the Jews. As a young man, just in his teens, God called him to be a prophet.

"Before I formed thee in the belly I knew thee; and before thou camest forth out of the womb I sanctified thee, and I ordained thee a prophet unto the nations" (Jer. 1:5). God was calling Jeremiah to be His prophet. He knew this young man. He knew He could trust him with truth.

But Jeremiah argued, "...Ah, Lord God! Behold, I cannot speak: for I am a child" (Jer. 1:6). The Lord encouraged him and assured him, "Be not afraid of their faces: for I am with thee to deliver thee..." (Jer. 1:8). And truly God was always with him.

However, he was a prophet who was rejected by his neighbors, his own family, the priests, other prophets, his friends, all of the people, and finally by the king.

And yet he is the prophet who painted such a beautiful picture of how the Lord desires to be in charge of our lives. The story of the potter's vessel (Jer. 18:1–6) describes how we can let go, and let God shape our destiny. "...Behold, as the clay is in the potter's hand, so are ye in mine hand, O house of Israel" (Jer. 18:6).

Jeremiah was the prophet who so plainly explained how to find God. "And ye shall seek me, and find me, when ye shall search for me with all your heart" (Jer. 29:13).

My friends and I often encourage each other by quoting Jeremiah 29:11 (NIV), which says, "For I know the plans I have for you," declares the Lord, "plans to prosper you and not to harm you, plans to give you hope and a future." God is always ready to forgive our sin and restore us to a heavenly health when we turn back to Him.

By taking in God's healing love, we can find hope and a future—no matter what our past. A new and noble life is available each day as we live within the plans God has for us.

God's amazing prophecies, rebukes, warnings, predictions, and promises were rejected. Therefore, the people and kings—yes, the entire nation of Israel got into terrible trouble for not accepting God's messages that Jeremiah's prophecies predicted.

In the very first chapter of the Old Testament book of Jeremiah, God warns Jeremiah he will have troubles, but God will be with him. "They will fight against you but will not overcome you, for I am with you and will rescue you" (Jer. 1:19, NIV).

Sure enough, he did get into trouble. He was beaten and put into stocks (Jer. 20:1), he was carried into Egypt (Jer. 43:5–7), and—worst of all— "they lowered him by ropes into the cistern" (Jer. 38:6, NIV).

A cistern is a well. But there was no water it. Only MUD. He sank down in the mud. Just think—the prophet of the Lord sinking down in MUD. Kind people eventually lifted him out with a rope. Yes, indeed God was with Jeremiah even when he was in the mire—the mud. And He is with you no matter where you are. His PRESENCE is promised. For He has plans for you, too.

Turn

While watching a breath-taking set of slides of nature at its best, I could hardly wait to meet the photographer. But after that incredible slide show, he was circled by too many people. And I was pushed for time to get to my next appointment. I was quite disappointed, because his slides not only showed flowers, trees, skies, baby animals, storms, oceans, rivers, waterfalls, and sunrises of all colors, but his narration revealed a wonderful character rarely found in a young man.

Many months later, he knocked on my door. Inviting him in, I wondered what his visit was all about. He was just travelling through my town and remembered I lived in that town. So he dropped in to say "hello."

Of course, we discussed the beauty of his pictures. He remarked, "Joy, you've just seen a few hundred. I've taken thousands and plan to continue using my camera for as long as I live."

Over a glass of lemonade, our conversation drifted from one subject to another, becoming friends in the process. Noticing his purity of speech, his innocent face, and the way he expressed himself, I realized I was in the presence of a young man who stood tall in character.

Curiosity got the best of me. I asked, "Well, what do you do if you have a temptation to sin?" I chuckled at his answer, "I grab my camera. I can spend an hour with a blade of grass, a dandelion, a leaf, or a bug, OR I can shoot the sky—and by then the temptation is gone."

The Bible gives the same formula for escaping temptation. TURN. The Message Bible puts it this way: "Tell them, 'As sure as I am the living God, I take no pleasure from the death of the wicked. I want the wicked to change their ways and live. Turn your life around! Reverse your evil ways! Why die, Israel?'" (Ezek. 33:11, TM).

That same verse in the King James Version of the Bible says, "...turn ye, turn ye from your evil ways; for why will ye die, O house of Israel?" Hosea 12:6 recommends, "Therefore turn thou to thy God...." Ezekiel 18:32 puts it this way, "...turn yourselves, and live ye."

Changing directions immediately gives a fresh start in life.

For me, when I'm tempted to do something I should not be doing, I have a great Bible text: 1 Corinthians 10:13: "There hath no temptation taken you but such as is common to man: but God is faithful, who will not suffer you to be tempted above that ye are able; but will with the temptation also make a way to escape, that ye may be able to bear it."

When we turn, we should look to Jesus—the only One who can make our lives good—here and now and forever.

Hebrews 12:2 says it so well, "Looking unto Jesus the author and finisher of our faith; who for the joy that was set before Him endured the cross, despising the shame, and is set down at the right hand of the throne of God."

That young man had it right when he turned from sin to a very good life. You can, too. TURN. Just turn.

Who Touched My Clothes?

Ten, tiny verses in the Holy Bible tell a special story for all of us. Twelve long years living with an unpopular illness. Spending all of her money on doctors who could not heal her. She didn't even have a name. Well, she did, but in the Bible, she remains nameless.

Twelve years—that's 144 months or 4,320 days (Jewish months had 30 days). That's a long, long time for a woman to bleed nonstop. Pain—physical, emotional, and social—was her lot for so long; it became a way of life. Doctors could not help her. She was called "unclean" and her energy level must have been very low.

The story starts out like this: "And a certain woman, which had an issue of blood twelve years..." (Mark 5:25). How humiliating! How humbling! How intrusive into her daily life!

The sad story continues (Mark 5:26) "...and had suffered many things of many physicians, and had spent all that she had, and was nothing bettered, but rather grew worse."

On top of all else, her finances were depleted. She was on the bottom of the heap of human tragedy. Talk about human morale hitting bottom— she lived on the bottom. Depression must have held her captive. Friends, one by one, must have deserted her long ago. Relatives, tired of her story, could not hold on to hope. I'd call this the bottom of the pits.

THEN JESUS CAME TO TOWN. Hope at last!

Jesus, our Healer, our Savior, and our closest Friend works invisibly. He heals and He saves. "When she had heard of Jesus," (Mark 5:27) "[she] came in the press behind, and touched his garment."

This is a great picture of what TRUST is. "For she said, 'If I may touch but His clothes, I shall be whole'" (Mark 5:28).

She had faith in this ONE DIVINE HEALER. And her faith in Jesus brought instant relief. Verse 29 shouts with victory: "And straightway the fountain of her blood was dried up; and she felt in her body that she was healed of that plague."

Fireworks of gratitude and relief had to be exploding in her inner person. Her faith in the Divine Healer activated healing in her body. She was well, free, whole, healed, changed in one moment, and she knew it.

> *Jesus, our Healer, our Savior, and our closest Friend works invisibly. He heals and He saves.*

She turned to go home. The thick mob of people was crushing her. As she turned to leave, she heard a voice—loud and clear. You see, Jesus also felt the change in Himself. He knew that, through Him, someone was healed. Actually, because Jesus was the "Son of Man" and the "Son of God"—both, born of Mary, yet God, Himself—He KNEW who had touched His garment.

Verse 30 says, "And Jesus, immediately knowing in himself that virtue had gone out of him, turned him about in the press, and said, 'WHO TOUCHED MY CLOTHES?' And his disciples…" (men no better and no worse than each of us—human beings) "…said unto him, 'Thou seest the multitude thronging thee, and sayest thou, Who touched me?'" (Mark 5:31) (emphasis added).

Jesus, our Healer, our Savior, and our closest Friend works invisibly. He heals, He saves, and He fills our hearts and minds without others peeking inside our inner parts to check up on what He is doing. No one in that huge crowd knew what need that one woman had—and no one could see her faith. Also, no one had a clue that Jesus had performed another miracle right there, right then. Yet the miracle took place right before their eyes. And they did not know.

Jesus and the woman knew it, though. "And he looked round about to see her that had done this thing" (Mark 5:32). Her heart must have pounded loudly in her ears.

She had just turned to go home quietly. But she realized she must admit her whole story. She had to tell her humiliating tale. She needed to thank the Healer. She was not used to speaking to a crowd of people.

Her heart must have been pounding, her fingers trembling, and her knees hardly able to hold her up. Embarrassment, frailty, fear of being found out, and yet excitement from the healing gripped her emotions like never before or ever after. The moment to decide to "come clean," to expose herself, had come. Wow!

Verse 33 goes on with the story. "But the woman fearing and trembling, knowing what was done in her, came and fell down before him, and told him all the truth."

Jesus has many ways to heal us. I often want to shout from the roof tops: "Jesus has healed me from my sins." But no, I just quietly live day by day, enjoying a simple life—the life of being forgiven. We all have the opportunity and choice to touch the hem of His garment. And we, too, shall be made whole.

Mark 5:34 wraps up this wonderful story in this way: "And he said unto her, Daughter, thy faith hath made thee whole; go in peace, and be whole of thy plague."

Trust. Faith. Healing. Think on these things.

The Rock of Surrender

Jesus knelt in the dirt and leaned on a large rock, asking His Father in heaven to "Let this cup pass from Me." The "cup" He was talking about was death on the cross of Calvary. He truly did not want to die. But His heart of love for each one of us was so strong, that He finally surrendered to the plan of salvation, saying, "...nevertheless not my will, but thine, be done" (Luke 22:42).

The rock of surrender is where He left His human will and accepted His destination of death on the cross. A few moments later, Judas arrived with a mob of soldiers and Jewish leaders. They came to capture Jesus, as if He were a criminal. The noise of their angry shouts woke Peter and all the disciples from their sleep.

Peter was horrified that his Master was the victim of this violence. In fact, he took his sword and cut off Malchus's ear. Quick-acting Peter was in trouble again. Jesus simply healed the servant's ear, as the angry mob watched.

The next thing Peter saw was his beloved Leader's hands being tied up as a criminal. Those in command, thrust Jesus forward to the high priest's palace. There, a mock trial led to a beating, cutting Jesus's back to shreds. Placing a crown of thorns on His head and mocking Him verbally added to the pain.

With horror, Peter watched from the warm fireside in the court yard. A young girl looked at Peter and said, "...This man was also with him" (Luke 22:56). Raw fear shuddered through his body, and he shouted, "Woman, I know Him not" (Luke 22:57). Later, Peter again denied his connection with the Man on trial.

The third time, another person said to Peter, "…Surely thou art one of them: for thou art a Galilaean, and thy speech agreeth thereto" (Mark 14:70). Then Peter lost all the goodness he had been trying to live up to. Denying Jesus, he cursed and swore saying, "I know not this man of whom ye speak" (Mark 14:71).

At that instant, a rooster crowed the second time. Jesus had predicted this would happen. Peter looked at Jesus who now turned and looked at him. A glance of Jesus's loving, forgiving look broke Peter's heart.

Peter ran out of the court yard, a truly broken man. Sobbing, he ran to the very rock of surrender Jesus had just left.

In her commentary about the life of Jesus, Ellen White wrote the following about Peter: "On the very spot where Jesus had poured out His soul in agony to His Father, Peter fell upon his face, and wished that he might die."3

Indeed, Peter fell on his knees just where Jesus's knees had been a few hours before. Peter was finally broken. Broken-hearted and broken in spirit. Jesus had not yet been crucified. The trial alone opened Peter's eyes. Peter saw himself for the first time for what he was—a bold, brash, self-willed sinner who needed a Savior. He, at last, recognized Jesus, the Son of God, as his Savior.

Jesus was just about to die a few hours later—for Peter and for all of us "self-willed Peters." Oh yes, I have recognized the "Peter personality" in my life, too.

This morning, I read 1 Peter 1 for my devotions. It occurred to me that a change in the heart and will of Peter came from that glance of love as the rooster crowed. His surrender followed at the very rock in the Garden of Gethsemane where Jesus had surrendered Himself as He prayed His "nevertheless" prayer.

As I read 1 Peter, chapter 1, I marveled at the complete change of heart Peter and all of us can have. Greatly rejoice—trial of your faith—more precious than gold—joy unspeakable—be sober—be obedient—be holy—these thoughts and much more in this chapter reveal the thinking of a truly changed man.

After Jesus died on the cross that Friday, He was resurrected three days later. Jesus had fulfilled the plan of salvation which was this: the cross, the tomb, the resurrection, and finally His ascension back to heaven.

This plan was set in heaven to save sinners and assure us of a home in heaven when He returns to take us home.

In Peter's second book in the Bible, we read, "The Lord knoweth how to deliver the godly out of temptations..." (2 Peter 2:9). A wonderful promise! Personally, I claim that promise a lot.

After his dramatic conversion, and, later at Pentecost where Peter and all the disciples received the Holy Spirit in tongues of fire (Acts 2:1–3), Peter preached to thousands about the cross of Calvary and why our Savior had to die for each of us.

In 2 Peter 1:3, we learn how we may have God's POWER over ALL sin: I especially like 2 Peter 1:3 (NIV): "His divine power has given us everything we need for life and goodness...."

I need and want that power. Don't you?

By Beholding

The most important day of our lives was the most challenging day for Jesus. The day He died, a mob of ruthless people shouted at Him with hating tongues, and, indeed, many terrible words and actions.

There were many different reactions as people "beheld" Jesus on the cross. The word behold means to have a "real awareness of what is seen."4

Nicodemus must have remembered his marvelous nighttime visit with Jesus many months before. Jesus told of God's love in John 3:16: "For God so loved the world, that he gave his only begotten Son, that whoso-ever believeth in him should not perish [die], but have everlasting life."

And this same Nicodemus, as well as Joseph of Arimathaea, buried the body of Jesus that very day. Mary, the mother of Jesus, could give birth to Him, but now she could not give life to Him. In her great agony, she just could not understand why her Son was dying.

Visualize this! Think about it for a bit. BEHOLD the LOVE that shone through the cross that Friday many years ago. The disciples were confused, saying, "...we trusted that it had been he which should have redeemed Israel..." (Luke 24:21).

The raging mob had looked without "beholding." They saw through impersonal and hateful eyes only. Their hearts were not "beholding."

But the thief on the cross beheld Jesus as the Savior. He alone recognized Christ's mission on earth: to die for OUR sins. He saw Jesus as HIS Savior. He pleaded, "...Lord, remember me when thou comest into thy kingdom" (Luke 23:42). He truly BEHELD Jesus for who He was: HIS Savior.

Others also believed. "And when the centurion...saw...[that he] gave up the ghost, he said, Truly this man was the Son of God" (Mark 15:39).

By beholding evil, we become more evil. By beholding Jesus Christ, we become heaven-bound.

HOW we look at the cross makes all the difference. By BEHOLD-ING, we become...your choice.

The Fire of Pentecost

Fire came down from heaven and entered the room where the disciples were praying. The fire separated into "tongues" of fire that were lit over the head of each of the 120 people gathered in the upper room (Acts 2:1–3).

Why were these 120 people gathered all in one room? Jesus, the Savior, had just finished His work on earth, had died on the cross, was resurrected from His tomb on the third day, and after forty days, He ascended back to heaven.

As they were talking of these events about Jesus, they had come together to think things through, to pray, and to let God purify their lives. Then, on the day of Pentecost, the FIRE came on each head.

There was POWER in that fire. It was then that the disciples fully understood Jesus's life and work on earth. Peter and the other disciples went about preaching to the huge group of people outside the room. Three thousand people were baptized in the name of the Father, Son, and Holy Spirit in just one day. Thousands turned to the Lord and in the days following, also.

What made the difference between Peter's brash tongue, James's and John's raging tempers, and Thomas's doubting nature? All the disciples were changed.

There was Holy Spirit POWER in the FIRE on the day of Pentecost.

The power of the Father, His Son, and His Spirit can change any of us. Why were these twelve disciples and the entire room of 120 people chosen as the channel for God's Spirit to work in the hearts of thousands in one day?

Because they were in "one accord in prayer" (Acts 1:14). Prayer is powerful. When two or three talk to God, things change. God knows the heart of each of us. He knows all our problems…what is in our hearts. He knows what to do for us, and when.

Wherever you are, whoever you are, whatever your dreams, God knows it all. He is beside you, ready to give you the right direction in your life. He knows your sorrows. There will be NO TEARS in heaven—all will finally be well. Be ready! Jesus WILL come back. He created YOU. He loves YOU. He wants to spend eternity with YOU.

A Throw-Away Girl

Deep in sin. Caught in the very act of sinning, Mary Magdalene was thrown down at Jesus's feet. The religious leaders were challenging Jesus with this problem. It was the law to stone a prostitute to death. And before Jesus's feet, Mary cowered in fear as Jesus agreed with the Jewish law (John 8:3–12).

> *As the eldest to the youngest read their own sins spelled out in the sand, they dropped their stones and left.*

But then He said, "...he that is without sin among you, let him first cast a stone at her" (John 8:7), and then He bent down to the ground and started writing. The men, curious to see what Jesus was writing, peered over their proud noses to read their own sins spelled out in the sand.

Yes, Jesus understood each accusing man's heart. As the eldest to the youngest read their own sins spelled out in sand, they dropped their stones and left (John 8:9).

Meanwhile, Mary was expecting the blows from the leaders who were just doing their duty. After all, the law required stoning for prostitution.

But wait—was there another solution to this problem? Could Jesus the Messiah have something better to offer Mary? Yes, He did. What He offered to Mary, He is offering it to each of us sinners: GRACE.

GRACE—Forgiveness and a promise.

Sitting at the Feet of Jesus

The disciples chose to ignore Jesus's story. In fact, they chose to be somewhere else. He tried three times to tell them about His crucifixion, but they were busy thinking about their "status" in His kingdom. Each wanted to be the greatest. Their egos just wouldn't let go.

Where the disciples were at the moment of this story, I don't know. But Jesus had a story to tell. There was only one person willing to hear. Indeed, she was the forgiven prostitute. As she sat at Jesus's feet, He explained about the cross. That very week, Jesus would be nailed to the cross. No one understood the story. Even Jesus's mother didn't understand about the cross.

But Jesus had one listener—Mary. She sat quietly as Jesus told His story—the most important story ever told. He laid out before Mary what would happen at the end of that week. She alone heard the story of the cross from the lips of the one Who would die on that Friday.

Mary alone received the blessing of those words. They are not recorded for us. It was a very private and personal conversation between Jesus and Mary.

Deep into the conversation, her sister Martha entered the room, scolding her because Mary was not in the kitchen helping. Now we DO know what Jesus said. He said, "…Martha, Martha, thou art careful and troubled about many things: But one thing is needful: and Mary hath chosen that good part, which shall not be taken away from her" (Luke:10:41–42).

Mary alone got the big picture of love.

The Alabaster Box

Gratitude overflowing Mary's heart, she looked for a way to honor her Master. The opportunity came at a banquet. Mark 14:3–9 tells this incredible love story. The book of John relates the same story in John 12:1–8.

Jesus was at a supper in the home of Simon, the leper. Mary's brother Lazarus was at the table, also. And of course, Mary's sister Martha served.

Simon who had had leprosy was healed, and he wanted to give this dinner in appreciation to honor Jesus who had healed him.

Lazarus, a special guest at the table, was deeply grateful to Jesus for giving life back to him, as Jesus had recently raised him from the dead. As Martha served, Mary had her own plan. She had found a way to thank and honor Jesus in a quiet manner.

Mary very quietly broke an alabaster box of ointment of spikenard—a very precious and costly perfume. She poured some of the ointment on Jesus's head and then knelt to anoint the feet of Jesus.

As she wiped Jesus's feet with her hair, the perfume filled the air, giving away her secret.

It seems when someone does a good deed, there's always a critic waiting to complain. Judas had his target. Jesus responded, "Let her alone." Mark 14:9 tells it this way: "Verily I say unto you, Wheresoever this gospel shall be preached throughout the whole world, this also that she hath done shall be spoken of for a memorial of her."

Costly ointment? I'd say priceless love.

At the Cross

"And many women were there beholding afar off, which followed Jesus from Galilee, ministering unto Him: among which was Mary Magdalene, and Mary the mother of James and Joses, and the mother of Zebedees children" (Matt. 27:55–56).

Such a pitiful few were willing to stand by Jesus in His worst moments. Again, we see Mary Magdalene, prominently positioned near the cross on Friday. She is mentioned along with the mother of James and Joses, Salome, and many other women (Mark 15:40–41).

> *Such a pitiful few were willing to stand by Jesus in His worst moments.*

Luke 23:49 mentions "…and the women that followed him from Galilee…."

John 19:25 states, "Now there stood by the cross of Jesus his mother, and his mother's sister, Mary the wife of Cleophas, and Mary Magdalene."

John, the disciple, was also standing there with Mary, the mother of Jesus. At one point, Jesus gave His mother to John, who later took her home and made a home for her in his own home (John 19:26–27).

Now picture this: five helpless women and John, who was Jesus's only disciple to stand by Him while He was on the cross. Love for Jesus was there, but such a pitiful few were willing to stand by Jesus in His worst moments. Their hearts were broken. After Jesus said, "It is finished," scripture says, "he bowed his head, and gave up the ghost" (John 19:30).

The sad group could do nothing. But two Pharisees, who secretly believed Jesus was the Messiah, came forth, asking to bury the body of

Jesus. And John, the only disciple there, helped Joseph of Arimathaea and Nicodemus lift Jesus's broken body from the cross, and they carried it to Joseph's tomb to lay it there to rest for the Sabbath. The depths of grief cannot be expressed.

But we find that Grace cannot be stopped. Jesus's death on Friday was not eternal. It was only the beginning. After Sabbath was over, the first day of the week came—we have a risen Savior who left us with a promise: Everlasting life (John 3:16).

At the Tomb

She who was forgiven much, loved much, and Jesus honored this love (John 20:1–18). After Sabbath, on the first day of the week, Mary Magdalene came to the tomb. The stone was rolled away, and the tomb was empty. Jesus was not there.

Crying, and strongly fearful that someone had stolen Jesus's body, Mary ran to Peter and John, saying, "They have taken away the Lord out of the sepulchre, and we know not where they have laid him." Mary's grief was inconsolable. Her Lord was gone.

Returning to the tomb, Mary looked into the tomb and saw two angels. They asked her why she was weeping. Still thinking someone stole the body of her Master, she turned away from the tomb.

Just outside the tomb was Someone. Still crying, she did not look up. If she had looked up, her joy would have burst forth. But, no. She had a few more moments of grief. She just assumed the Man was the gardener.

"Jesus said unto her, Woman, why weepest thou? whom seekest thou? She, supposing him to be the gardener, saith unto him, Sir, if thou have borne him hence, tell me where thou hast laid him, and I will take him away" (John 20:15).

Nothing could soothe her grief. She could hardly breathe, she was so sad. Nothing could help—until Jesus breathed her name.

He just said, "MARY" (John 20:16) (emphasis added). That one word was enough to fill her heart with joy!

God's Incredible Plan for You

God is not sorry He made you. He has plans for you. Silently, tell Him your story; He can read your mind. Remember, God created your brain. God specializes in being close to people behind bars. No matter where you are or what you have done, God really does have plans for you.

> *God specializes in being close to people behind bars. No matter where you are or what you have done, God really does have plans for you.*

The crush of noise, the silence of solitude, the pain of body or emotions, or even honest guilt is prison enough. In some ways, we all have a touch of prison-life. The truth is—God specializes in being close to people behind bars.

No matter WHERE you are or WHAT you have done, God really does have plans for you. "For I know the plans I have for you…," He says in Jeremiah 29:11 (NIV), "…plans to prosper you and not to harm you, plans to give you hope and a future."

Jesus stands at the door of your heart just waiting to hear you say, "Come in. You are welcome in My heart." JOY and PEACE walk in with Him. They accompany the presence of the Lord—no matter where you live. Jesus is GOD'S INCREDIBLE LOVE. John 3:16 (NIV) says, "For God so loved the world that he gave his one and only Son, that whoever believes in him shall not perish but have eternal life." Whoever means YOU.

Eugene Peterson's The Message puts it this way: "This is how much God loved the world: He gave his Son, his one and only Son. And this is why: so that no one need be destroyed; by believing in him, anyone can have a whole and lasting life..." (John 3:16, TM).

John 3:17 (TM) goes on to assure us: "God didn't go to all the trouble of sending his Son merely to point an accusing finger, telling the world how bad it was. He came to help, to put the world right again."

But, you may be wondering, what about my crimes—and my sins? Well, just let Him into your heart. Tell him your story. He knows how to forgive. Actually He did that already at the cross. In 1 John 1:9, His promise to us is this: "If we confess our sins, he is faithful and just to forgive us our sins, and to cleanse us from all unrighteousness."

Jesus is ALWAYS at the door of your heart, waiting to come in. He assures us: "Lo, I am with you always..." (Matt. 28:20).

In time, JOY will shine on your face, and PEACE will grow in your heart. You really can live in His plan of LOVE right where you are, right now!

Trapped in Neutral?

No matter where you are, your self is always with you. Sounds a bit crazy, but wait. Each human on earth is different, unique from all other humans, including twins. Even the Dionne quintuplets, born in 1934, each had special and separate personalities and character traits.

Our journey in life is so special that no one can take you away from yourself. And yet no matter where we are in life, each of us, at some time in our life experience, finds ourselves trapped in neutral.

Stuck—can't seem to move. Feeling helpless as the world is whizzing by and you're standing still. Whoa! There must be something to break this neutral and truly boring experience.

My friends tell me, "Joy, you always turn to God for solutions to your problems." Maybe they are right. And it does work for me. More and more, as I turn to the Lord for help with ANY problem, big or tiny, I have more confidence that life situations turn out for the good, after all. And you, too, can experience this! So, I'm happy to share with you some Bible texts that take me "out of neutral" and into a "better thinking mode," resulting in a better living lifestyle. Here are some great thoughts from God's own word, the Bible.

Romans 8:28. "And we know that all things work together for good to them that love God, to them who are called according to his purpose."

Job 23:10. "But he knoweth the way that I take: when he hath tried me, I shall come forth as gold."

Psalm 48:14. "For this God is our God for ever and ever: he will be our guide even unto death."

Psalm 18:29. "For by thee I have run through a troop; and by my God have I leaped over a wall."

Psalm 20:7. "Some trust in chariots, and some in horses: but we will remember the name of the Lord our God."

Psalm 23:1. "The Lord is my shepherd; I shall not want."

Jeremiah 1:8. "Be not afraid of their faces: for I am with thee to deliver thee, saith the Lord."

Jeremiah 17:14. "Heal me, O Lord, and I shall be healed; save me, and I shall be saved; for thou art my praise."

Ezekiel 36:26. "A new heart also will I give you, and a new spirit will I put within you: and I will take away the stony heart out of your flesh, and I will give you an heart of flesh."

Matthew 19:26. "But Jesus beheld them, and said unto them, With men this is impossible; but with God all things are possible."

Matthew 26:41. "Watch and pray, that ye enter not into temptation: the spirit indeed is willing, but the flesh is weak."

Luke 23:34. "Then said Jesus, Father, forgive them; for they know not what they do…."

In talking about the future, we have another great promise: "And God shall wipe away all tears from their eyes; and there shall be no more death, neither sorrow, nor crying, neither shall there be any more pain…" (Rev. 21:4).

Running Away

When we have run away, which way should we look? Do we look to God who loves us and is right there with us? Or do we choose to look the other way and miss the blessing?

The very first man who ever lived ran away from God. He did wrong and was afraid to face his Creator.

> *When we have run away, which way should we look? Do we look to God who loves us and is right there with us? Or do we choose to look the other way and miss the blessing?*

In the cool of the evening, the Lord was in the habit of visiting Adam and Eve in the Garden of Eden. They walked and talked together and enjoyed nature in its most pristine glory. Then one day, Adam did something wrong, and he and his wife hid from God that evening. God found him and challenged him. His response was to blame his wife (Gen. 3:8–12).

Later in the Bible, Hagar, Abram's concubine, ran away when Sarai was treating her so harshly. Scripture tells the story so well: "And the angel of the Lord found her by a fountain of water in the wilderness,... And he said, Hagar, Sarai's maid, whence camest thou? and whither wilt thou go? And she said, I flee from the face of my mistress Sarai" (Gen. 16:7–8).

Verse 13 shows us that she finally realized Who she was talking with. "...Thou God seest me..." When we run from our troubles, we can also say, "Thou God seest me."

Later in earth's history, a young man named Jacob ran away from his angry brother. He was afraid, because he knew he had done something wrong. Fear-driven, he ran many miles from home. Exhausted, he fell asleep in a wild country. Using a rock for a pillow, he dreamed about a ladder reaching up to heaven with angels going up and down on that ladder. When he woke up, amazement filled his heart. Jacob felt the forgiving presence and love that God had for him and God has for each of us when we run away.

Genesis 28:16 puts it this way, "And Jacob awaked out of his sleep, and he said, Surely the Lord is in this place; and I knew it not."

Later, this same Jacob wrestled all night with the Angel of the Lord. At dawn, the heavenly "wrestler" touched Jacob's thigh, making it go out of joint. In his pain, Jacob now realized Who he was fighting. Jacob's response was, "...I will not let thee go, except thou bless me" (Gen. 32:26).

Years later, Jacob's son, Joseph, was innocent, but his brothers were jealous of him. His ten older brothers threw him in a pit to die. Later, taking him out of the pit, they sold him to people in a caravan travelling to Egypt.

In Egypt, he was sold as a slave. Circumstances took him from one tough spot to another. When trapped in a temptation, he ran away saying, "...how then can I do this great wickedness, and sin against God?" (Gen. 39:9).

Landing in prison, though he did no wrong, he stayed faithful to the Lord. God had His eye upon this young man. By and by, he was made governor of Egypt.

Another Bible story tells how God handpicked Moses to lead the children of Israel out of bondage, but, when he was forty years old, he killed a man and had to run away. He hid himself with a family in another country for forty more years. When he was eighty years old, God called Moses back to Egypt to be the leader of His chosen people.

The great exodus of Israel moving out of Egypt and into the Promised Land was an awesome journey. Moses, the meekest man on earth, now led millions on a forty-year wilderness trip. Finally, Israel came to Canaan, the Promised Land.

A different example of running was when David was still very young, and he ran TOWARD the enemy, Goliath. With a stone in his slingshot, he killed Israel's enemy and cut off his head. David did not run away, but toward, Goliath.

But soon after, David ran away from King Saul, whose jealousy was so intense that he craved David's life. Yes, David ran a lot, and yet God had His hand over him. After years of running away, David finally became King of Israel. God was his Protector.

Another example happened when, after a very dramatic confrontation for the Lord on Mount Carmel (1 Kings 18:20–40), Elijah's prayer to the living God brought down fire on the altar before the priests of Baal. But later, Elijah ran away because Jezebel, the queen, threatened to kill him. Then Elijah ran for his life. He ran all day (1 Kings 19: 1–3).

Exhausted, he fell down in sleep. An angel woke him and fed him. He slept again. After more sleep and more food, he traveled forty days and forty nights. Living in a cave, Elijah was visited by God Himself. The wind, the earthquake, and the fire were awesome to experience. But after all of that, God came to Elijah in a "still small voice" (God often comes to His people even today in a still small voice (1 Kings 19:5–12). What a beautiful connection.

In another example from the Old Testament, God asked Jonah to prophesy to Nineveh. He ran in the other direction, boarded a ship, was caught in a storm, was finally thrown into the sea where he was swallowed by a great fish. There, he had three days of solitude to think about what God really wanted from him. He reluctantly obeyed. And the whole town turned to the Lord because of Jonah delivering God's message.

In the New Testament, when Jesus lived on earth, two men ran away— one to his death and one to his own salvation. Judas betrayed Jesus with a kiss; later, he ran away and hanged himself. Peter heard the rooster crow. It broke his heart. He ran to Gethsemane, and, crying with bitter tears, became a changed man. Now, with his life in God's hands, the Father could use him to win people's hearts for eternal life. Two opposite responses, two different eternal destinations.

At the end of the road, when we have run away, which way should we look? Up to God who loves us and is right there with us? Or do we choose to look the other way and miss the blessing?

My prayer is that you will choose this way: "Yes, my soul, find rest in God; my hope comes from him" (Ps. 62:5, NIV).

The Best Day

Write it on your heart that every day is the best day of the year. Yesterday may have been a terrible day for you. The past cannot be changed. But today is still in YOUR power. Forgive yourself. Ask God to forgive you. And move on.

You are wiser today than you were yesterday, as you admit you have done wrong. There is no human who is without flaws. Each of us would like to erase part of the past, because we do not live in a faultless world.

Consider this. We don't get to choose how we are going to die or when that will happen, but we can decide now how we are going to live each day.

When I was a senior in high school, my piano teacher said, "Joy you will never be a piano player." It may had been an "off" day for her, so I looked at her in surprise. I thought "I've just played The Flight of the Bumblebee by Rimsky-Korsakov. What does she mean I can't play the piano? I'll show her!"

No human is perfect. But within each of us is a spark of something we can do well.

Learning to play the piano is a long process that is filled with mistakes. But practicing each day irons out these mistakes, and, by recital time, near perfect music happens. The parents smile. The teacher is relieved, and the student enjoys that applause. Growing into a good piano player involves baby steps at first, but then, gradually, complex and truly beautiful music comes as a result.

Start to act as if it is impossible to fail anymore. I still hear one of my college roommates tell me, "Joy, rise above it," when things went very badly one day.

One of the greatest pleasures in life is doing something people say you cannot do. Ah yes, I have played the piano for 80 years. And I have taught hundreds of students how to play the piano—this became my life work.

Ida Scott Taylor wrote this little poem:

"One day at a time—
this is enough.
Do not look back and grieve over the past,
for it is gone;
And do not be troubled
about the future,
for it has not yet come.
Live in the present,
And make it so beautiful
That it will be worth
Remembering."5

Yes. In knowing that we can't change the PAST, we could ruin a perfectly good PRESENT by worrying about the FUTURE.

Opportunities to grow come in many forms. Surprise someone with a touch of kindness, maybe even a smile. The golden thread that binds humanity to itself is through kindness. Kindness is also a character trait of God. The Lord says in Jeremiah 31:3: "…I have loved thee with an everlasting love: therefore with lovingkindness have I drawn thee."

Kindness is a form of love. People who deserve love the least are really people who need it most. Smile—be kind—share a good word. Encourage a sad person. WOW! This is a great way to make the Best Day for someone else. And the glow in your life will be awesome.

"This is the day which the Lord hath made; we will rejoice and be glad in it (Ps. 118:24).

We all need love and encouragement; this is something we never outgrow. Give kindness—and a smile—you'll never regret it.

Have the BEST DAY—today. God bless you!

I Promise You

"And God shall wipe away all tears from their eyes; and there shall be no more death, neither sorrow, nor crying, neither shall there be any more pain…" (Rev. 21:4). What a powerful promise. The need for tears will be wiped away.

John, the revelator, gave us hope in a future eternal life in heaven, by describing what will NOT be there. Within that description is the promise of a future home in heaven with a wonderful, beautiful, perfect, and satisfying life—forever!

When God says, "I promise you," He is true to His word. He follows through. But it's also true that you can turn your back on God and miss out on the blessing. The prophet Jeremiah speaks for God when he says, "…your sins have withheld good from you" (Jer. 5:25, AMP). But God has so much to offer every human being; it would be a shame to turn down His blessings.

Paul tells us in Romans 4:21, "… what he had promised, he was able also to perform." We can have utmost confidence in God's promises. In 2 Peter 1:4, Peter calls God's promises "…exceeding great and precious promises…."

These two great men of God, Peter and Paul, had flawed characters before God entered their lives in a very dramatic manner. Each man gave his heart to the Lord and came through the conversion process totally changed, and they became reliable workers for the Lord. Their turn-around life was complete. They could talk and write about their Lord with such conviction that thousands accepted Jesus Christ as their Savior.

And "…weeping may endure for a night but joy cometh in the morning" (Ps. 30:5). Tears—a good cry—can do as much good for us as a good hot shower or a cozy bath. They both clean away the dirt of the past and bring relief for the future. A good cry releases and washes away the burden on the soul. King David, who wrote the psalms, cried often. He knew the value of tears.

Before Jesus was crucified, He talked to His disciples (and to all of us) in John 14:2, assuring them and us that "In my Father's house are many mansions....I go to prepare a place for you." That's what He is doing for us right now, building our heavenly home. What a PROMISE!

Romans 8:28 is an encouraging promise from the Lord, "And we know that all things work together for good to them that love the Lord...." In my darkest experiences in life, I always wondered how God would take these and work them "for good." Later, when I would look back, I could see God's hand in every experience. I am frequently in awe of God's methods.

A friend of mine has a very difficult job and an even more difficult home life. I have asked, "How do you hold up?" His answer is, "My grace is sufficient for thee," quoting 2 Corinthians 12:9. What great trust in God's promises!

John 3:16 is a very famous Bible promise. But we seem to overlook John 3:17, which assures us, "For God sent not his Son into the world to condemn the world; but that the world through him might be saved." By turning our complete trust to Jesus Christ our Savior, we are safe. God did not say, "No troubles." He said, "No condemnation" (Rom. 8:1).

God has prepared "a way to escape" when we are tempted to sin. The promise in 1 Corinthians 10:13 goes this way: "There hath no temptation taken you but such as is common to man: but God is faithful, who will not suffer [let] you to be tempted above that ye are able; but will with the temptation also make a way to escape, that ye may be able to bear it."

King Solomon, the wisest person who ever lived, expressed one of God's many promises this way: "I love them that love me; and those that seek me early shall find me" (Prov. 8:17), which is a great reason to worship the Lord first thing in the morning.

James, the stepbrother of Jesus, advises, "Submit yourselves therefore to God. Resist the devil, and he will flee from you" (James 4:7).

When God says, "I promise you," His promise can be counted on!

Will You Give God a Chance?

God takes the rap for a lot of things. Many people ask, "Where is God?" Some people ask, "Who is God?" Others ask, "What is God doing with my life?" or "Why did my favorite person die?" or "How could the great God of the universe look down on the earth and watch so much tragedy? Will it end? And WHEN will it end?"

Fortunately, there will be a "last day" on earth, a day when tragedies no longer exist. Yes, there is a God. Scientists and many other people try to explain Him away. They are wrong. There IS a God. He is NOT Santa Claus. He is our CREATOR. There is also a devil called Satan. And Satan is a created being—a fallen angel—who was first known as Lucifer.

Lucifer became jealous of God. He foolishly wanted to BE God. He desired the worship only God deserved. Because he stirred up trouble in heaven, God finally had to kick Lucifer out of Heaven, and Lucifer's name was changed to Satan. That started the greatest debate in the universe.

Political debate is mild compared to the "great debate" between God and Satan. After God created the earth, crafty Satan enticed Adam and Eve to turn their loyalty to him and away from God. Thus the "great controversy" between good and evil took over the land.

The battle between God and Satan continues on and on and is growing stronger every day. Death, abuse, and calamities of all kinds daily shock each of us. And it grows worse and worse. No wonder so many people wonder, "Is someone in charge?" Fortunately, God has already won the victory at the cross over 2,000 years ago. We have a Savior who took our sins upon Himself, died for our sins, was resurrected from death, ascended back to His home in heaven, and promised His disciples—you and me—He will return to receive us and take us to His home: Heaven.

When? He said, "Soon." No one knows the time or day. However, the promise is a perfect promise. He IS coming.

Fortunately for us all, there is no sin too big for God to forgive.

This is where you and I have a vote about where we will go. "...We have a hell to shun and a heaven to win."6 "...Choose you this day whom ye will serve... (Josh. 24:15).

Grace and mercy describe the act of Jesus's dying on the cross for our sins. "For God so loved the world, that he gave his only begotten Son, that whosoever believeth in him should not perish, but have everlasting life" (John 3:16). And John 3:17 says, "For God sent not his Son into the world to condemn the world; but that the world through him might be saved."

> *Fortunately for us all, there is no sin too big for God to forgive. Living in this prison on earth, we CAN be free.*

Fortunately for us all, there is no sin too big for God to forgive. Living in this prison on earth, we CAN be free. Before Jesus, our Lord, was born, the angel told Mary's husband Joseph in a dream, "...thou shalt call His name Jesus: for he shall save his people from their sins" (Matt. 1:21). Notice that they were saved from"—NOT saved in"—their sins.

This saving called "salvation" covers all of US and ALL sin. We are ALL forgiven and loved by God our Father, Jesus His Son, and Their Spirit, the Holy Spirit. But it is necessary for you to ASK for forgiveness of sin. At that moment, you are forgiven. In fact, on the cross YOU (and all of us) were already forgiven. That is the very reason He died—to forgive our sin and win a heavenly home for us.

With God inviting us to His side and the devil trying to entice us to "worship" or "honor" him, we have a choice to make: Join God, or join Satan. Choosing God is making the best of a difficult and painful life. Living in this prison on earth, we CAN be free. "For by grace are ye saved through faith....it is the gift of God" (Eph. 2:8).

It is through the eyes of faith that we find meaning in the middle of our bitterest pain. Faith in God frees our inner person and gives us JOY. I desire to choose God. I pray you do, too.

God is ready for you. Are you ready for Him? Will you give God a chance?

Encouraging Words

"Alone" is a dreadful word. But "…lo, I am with you…" (Matt. 28:20) is a promise from Jesus Christ Himself. This promise changes "me" to "we." It takes us from "alone" to "together."

You don't have to be behind bars to experience solitary times; there is no human being or earthly possession that can fill the emptiness for us. Only God can do that. And when He finally fills your heart and mind, you realize you never need to be "all alone" again.

I believe that you are never out of God's mind. After all, God created each of us, so He continues to love us and watch us grow in His Presence. The Eternal Father loves us like a Shepherd loves each of His sheep. When one is hurt, He heals it. If it is lost, He looks for it and finds it. Oh yes, we are NEVER out of God's mind.

We human beings are incurably "religious." We need Someone bigger than we are to look up to. After trying alcohol, drugs, and excitement of all kinds—even after worshipping idols of every kind known to man, there is still a tug in the heart and mind that says, "TRY GOD."

Once you "try God," you find that "…the God who started this great work in you would keep at it and bring it to a flourishing finish on the very day Christ Jesus appears" (Phil. 1:6, TM).

"God himself is present in you…" (1 Cor. 3:16, TM). The Holy Spirit is a guide who "…will make everything plain to you….I don't leave you the way you're used to being left—feeling abandoned…" (John 14:26, 27, TM).

So, once we have accepted Christ as our Savior, His Spirit lives in us. The Holy Spirit is a guide who teaches about God's plans for us. That terrible emptiness is gone. The Holy Spirit fills our hearts and minds with the love of Jesus. Jesus, filling us with His Spirit, becomes closer to us than any human being on earth. The toys and trinkets of this earth are empty in comparison.

And there is more—much more. The promise, " ...lo, I am with you always..." (Matt. 28:20) includes eternal life after death. Life—the best now, and life forever. God's presence ALWAYS and even for eternity.

Sometimes we feel we have sinned too much and messed up our lives beyond even God's help. But take heart! Jesus said, "...with God all things are possible" (Matt. 19:26). If you do sin, grab your Bible, God's word, and read these verses.

"And we know that all things work together for good to them that love God..." (Rom. 8:28).

"For God sent not his Son into the world to condemn the world; but that the world through him might be saved" (John 3:17).

Even King David declared: "Whither shall I go from thy spirit? Or whither shall I flee from thy presence?" (Ps. 139:7).

In 1 Corinthians 10:13, we are told, "There hath no temptation taken you but such as is common to man: but God is faithful, who will not suffer you to be tempted above that ye are able; but will with the temptation also make a way to escape, that ye may be able to bear it."

The longer I live, the more important that text is to me. A WAY TO ESCAPE. There seems to be just a moment before the decision to sin. In that moment, I'm learning to send a quick prayer to God: "HELP ME!" He always comes up with the way to escape THAT sin. Sometimes, I forget this formula, so I go ahead and sin, but then immediately regret it. I'm glad to say there's big improvement in my life in this area. Not perfect yet, but grateful for that "way out."

But if we do sin again, we have a beautiful assurance that, "If we confess our sins, he is faithful and just to forgive us our sins..." He will also clean us up fresh all over again: the text continues to say, "...and to cleanse us from all unrighteousness" (1 John 1:9).

Jesus will never reject anyone. His own words in John 6:37 (AMP) assure us, "...I will never, no never reject one of them who comes to Me." That same verse in the New International Bible encourages us this way: "...whoever comes to me I will never drive away."

In John, chapter 8, there is a story about Mary, who was caught sinning. I love my Savior a little more each time I read the story and hear His wonderful words: "Neither do I condemn you" (John 8: 11, NIV).

"You will seek me and find me when you seek me with all your heart" (Jer. 29:13, NIV). Salvation is a gift freely given at the cross of Christ (an act called "GRACE").

Soon this old, flawed earth will take a change with even worse things to come. When things get so bad, Jesus will return to our earth. He will raise the faithful to new life, and together we will ascend into heaven, for a life free of sin and pollution. As John said in Revelation 22:20, "Even so, come, Lord Jesus." I often think of running into the safe arms of Jesus.

Dear reader, I hope to see you when we all get to heaven.

The Power of Love

There are many stories about the love that people have for birds. I remember hearing about a cardinal that was injured. Someone rescued it, but the love continued as seven birds circled it, bringing food to the bird as it recovered. LOVE is truly powerful, even with animals.

Human love is only a small taste of love compared to Divine love. I have a friend who changes diapers for her baby, as well as for her aging mother. Only pure love can keep her singing, as she does. Another friend tends a beautiful garden, cared for with obvious love for her gorgeous flowers. She gives lovely bouquets to shut-ins nearly every day. There is power in this love.

> *Human love is only a small taste of love compared to Divine love.*

Human love is only a small taste of love compared to Divine love. It was pure love that kept Jesus on course, as days, weeks, months, and years ticked off, all pointing forward to the cruel cross. Staying on that cross was the strongest gift of love given to mankind. The power of the cross comes from that love.

Peter's denial of his Lord at the trial in Pilate's court brought forth a LOOK OF LOVE from the Savior's eyes. That look broke Peter's heart, and he never again was the brash, bold, self-sufficient person as before that "LOOK OF LOVE." In fact, he wrote two books in the New Testament: 1 Peter and 2 Peter. An incredible example of how deeply his life was changed. I've just re-read 2 Peter through again, and I am amazed at his grasp of God's plan.

When moms and dads rear their children with love in their hearts, that's powerful. I well remember my Dad's loving eyes, the look of disappointment when I "blew it again," yet an assurance of love, even when I disobeyed.

Jesus's advice to "love your enemies" is a very difficult path to take; yet it's the best decision. Indeed, the test of truly belonging to the Lord is found in John 13:35. "By this shall all men know that ye are my disciples, if ye have love one to another."

Hatred, the opposite of love, can only make your inner self die a slow and lonely death. Cain, the very first man born on earth, hated his brother, Abel, so completely, that he killed him (Gen. 4:1–8).

Esau and Jacob were twin brothers. After Jacob stole the blessing from Esau, he had to leave his home for safety reasons, never again to see his beloved mother. Esau's hatred was so strong that the family was never happy again (Gen. 27:41–43).

The hatred of many Jewish rulers for the Savior drove Him to the cross. Hatred is never good. It always puts the "hater" as well as the "hated" under the control of the devil. Love, forgiving love, divine love (called agape) is the only solution to erase hatred and embrace love.

"Who shall separate us from the love of Christ? ...[Nothing] shall be able to separate us from the love of God, which is in Christ Jesus our Lord (Rom. 8:35–39).

Trust God's love for you. Then share it with others.

The Pity Party

I was crying my heart out. I was angry, and I didn't know what to do. But I had a meeting to attend, and, as deeply distressed as I was, I threw myself in the car and drove to the meeting. I don't know how much good I was for anyone else, but I did learn one important lesson that day.

Swallowing my tears and stifling my smoldering emotions, I finally turned to the person next to me, whom I had seen for the first time that afternoon. She apparently had her own issues because she hadn't even looked at me either. But about one-half hour after the meeting started, we locked eyes in surprise.

During the intermission, I confessed what was troubling me. I was having a pity-party. My new friend, Betty, listened to me as I belched out my anger and a big hunk of loneliness. I was crying loudly by now. All of a sudden, she smiled, and she told me a joke.

Just as hard as I had been crying, I started laughing. At that moment, I realized how silly it is to have a pity-party that is all my own. Betty told me more. I have followed her advice ever since.

She said, "Remember twenty. Twenty seconds, twenty minutes, twenty hours, twenty days, twenty weeks, twenty months, twenty years." All that feeling sorry for yourself adds up. Self-pity needs to be released.

We all need sympathy from time to time. And when there is no one giving this sympathy, we MUST give it to ourselves. Thus, the private pity-party serves its purpose. The question is: How long should a one-person pity-party last? I now choose to set my timer for twenty minutes. I sit down and have my own pity party and feel sorry for "poor little Joy." Then, when the timer dings, I clap my hands, get up, and walk forward to have a good life for the rest of the day!

Betty and I talked a long time about resentment. I had never paid attention to the word resentment before. She explained that even though a person had a calm exterior, there is often an inner anger within the mind and heart—called resentment. And even if I refused to lash out with anger, I had frozen anger within me that I didn't even realize. FROZEN ANGER. A new thought to me, but that was where I had lived all my life.

This very morning, I was left alone with another bout of resentment that threatened to destroy my day. I took time out to set the timer, sit down, and "enjoy" a pity-party all my own. I have learned that twenty minutes is adequate for me. I just pour sympathy all over myself for twenty minutes (no one else knows or even cares). When the timer bell rings, I clap my hands, stand up, stretch my arms up to the ceiling, relax, and go on to a good, new beginning—LIFE!

After that, I started singing. Sing away the blues. It works. And it brings cheer to others along the way.

Proverbs 15:13 says, "A merry heart maketh a cheerful countenance...." That's right!

Become...

Twin boys, Tommy and Danny, were fun-loving boys. Oh, how they loved to play jokes on people. They had a language all their own. When they were three years old, it rained a lot that year, so they played in the house nearly every day. Their mother had her hands full, as playing jokes on her was their only source of real entertainment, except the TV.

In the first grade, Danny got blamed for the mischief. Tommy had a sly way of looking like he was innocent, and he did not get into trouble as much. Tommy had a way of looking at his twin, always getting Danny to follow through with the mischief.

As one year passed another year, grade school, then high school, and even college, the twins got much better at doing things that got them into trouble. However, Danny also learned to be much more sly, and so the mystery of their trouble-making went unsolved. They both learned to deal undercover. Slight tricks with their hands, a wink, a nod of the head, and many other clever devices finally got the boys into big trouble.

As the twins grew from cute little boys into devil-may-care men, the excitement of crime became their way of life. One night, about 2 a.m., their life of crime came to an end. A flashlight shining in their faces didn't even give them a chance to run this time. They were caught. They were thrown in jail that very night, and, when the time came, they were sentenced.

A wise judge sent these fellows to two different prisons. Now for the first time, Danny had a chance to stand on his own two feet. He drifted toward a small group of fellow inmates who had a different look on their faces. The hard lines of evil seemed to soften when they saw each other.

Danny became curious about this small group. He finally joined them one night in a prayer group. He was drawn toward their unusual attitudes within the larger group—all of whom were behind bars.

Tommy, on the other hand, was delighting in the company of inmates who loved to plan crime, and who planned how to do the next job, as soon as they might be released. The "time" for Tommy was not much longer, and he learned as much about crime as he could. Finally the day arrived for his release.

It didn't take him long to get into trouble once again. This time, his sentence was for life.

Meanwhile, Danny was given a Bible. He had "time on his hands," and he read the Book. He started reading Mark—a short book on the life of his Savior, Jesus Christ. As his curiosity got the best of him, he kept reading. Soon, he prayed the sinner's prayer. Soon he was comfortable and at home now with his "Bible friends."

By and by, Danny walked out of prison. By "BEHOLDING," Danny became changed. Today, he is a loving family man, doing well with his life. No, life isn't easy for him, but life is really never easy for anyone. By and by, he visited his mom, taught her about his new-found Savior, prayed with her, and saw a change in her, too.

This is a success story about one man. It is also a tragic story for his twin. By beholding, they each became...CHANGED.

Three Pouts and a Smile

Three children pouted as they passed me. I had just opened the door to the party, and I was looking forward to a great and entertaining evening. My mood was interrupted from the joy I had had while I was preparing for this event. I had dressed, driven over, and parked in the driveway of this lovely home, and nearly danced up the steps. Now, all this pouting stopped me in my tracks. But I noticed there really was a party mood inside the large room ahead of me.

A man, wheeling his wheelchair toward me, flashed a smile in my direction. He invited me in with his eyes, and his excitement about seeing me was obvious. Ahh! The party had begun. It began with that smile. Realizing that the three pouting girls were "in one of those moods," I allowed this man's smile to warm me—to fill me with joy for the evening ahead.

A smile, the value is priceless. No matter our condition, such as this man in a wheelchair, or wherever you are—possibly behind bars—a smile can make the difference to someone, as this smile did for me.

My name is "Joy." My cousin, Linda, calls me "Joyful Joy." And for the most part, I'm certain she has named me well. Sometimes, I say twisted sentences that friends tease me about. Years ago, I told a friend, "I'm going to get car in my gas." Just last week, I warned a friend, "Don't hatch your chickens." YOU know that I meant, "Don't count your chickens before they are hatched." But now, I'm blushing over my friendly faux pas. It's so much easier to write than to speak. I can edit any word and make it come out better than in the first draft. By now, I know that you're smiling at my expense, but I'm realistic. You can laugh at me, because I laugh at myself, too!

Perhaps this is the very reason I love children so much. Indeed, teaching piano lessons brings forth many anxieties during a lesson, as the student complains about school, the teacher, math, or shares home trauma. I listen and then give some happy thoughts that brings a smile. Tears and laughter balance any situation.

I visit nursing homes often. Playing the piano brings smiles to the faces of the wheelchair-bound people. Often, if I play "The Old Rugged Cross" or "I Come to the Garden Alone," the people sing along. They know the words. And the nurses shake their heads in astonishment, because many of the residents of the nursing home don't talk anymore, but just watch them sing an old favorite hymn—now THAT brings a big smile to my face.

If you have found the Lord behind bars, I'm certain that at times others question if your glow—your smile—is for real. But no matter where we are, God is there. Let that be your anchor today as you face difficult people and situations.

By and by, the Lord is really coming to receive His people and take them to a better life. This is no lie. Revelation, chapters 21 and 22 describe heaven, God's home, where He is building YOUR home right now. Jesus said, "Let not your heart be troubled....In my Father's house are many mansions.... I go and prepare a place for you.... I will come again, and receive you unto myself; that where I am, there ye may be also" (John 14:1–3.) That should put a smile on your face!

Our future life will be much better than life as it is here now. Be faithful to your Lord, give HIM a smile. Know that He is smiling down at you.

Travelling to London

Taking the plane from Albuquerque, New Mexico, to the Dallas/Fort Worth airport in Texas was the easy part. Catching the plane to London was my nightmare.

Six months earlier, Shirley and I were music teachers and performers in a week-long choral and piano festival for nearly a hundred high school boys and girls from all over New Mexico. We were given a lovely guest room in the girls' dormitory. Each night after intensive teaching and performing music, we collapsed in our own beds, turned the lights out, and started talking. As the week progressed, chitchat and laughter became more serious talk, and, by Thursday night, we were good "new" friends.

Shirley had been in Europe six times and mentioned that she was a good guide. So when she got through painting mental pictures of the delight of travel around Europe, I sleepily murmured, "Yeah, Shirley. That would be fun," and went to sleep.

Three months later, Shirley called me on the phone and said, "I bought the tickets!" She gave me the dates and asked me to pay her back. Meanwhile, my Uncle Harold died, leaving me a bit of money and well, yes indeed, this was the trip of a lifetime, and I could then afford it.

She assured me she would meet me in Texas as I came off the airplane.

A few weeks later, she called me late at night, changing our plans. Instead of meeting me at my plane from Albuquerque, she asked if possibly I could meet her at the plane going to London. I went right back to sleep. I should have written a note about the change. Oops!

As I got off my plane from Albuquerque, I was only thinking about plan ONE. I looked around for Shirley. No Shirley. I had her paged. No Shirley. I waited a bit, as I had four hours to wait. Then my memory went, "Ding-dong, Joy. Now what was that late-night phone call about?"

I asked the ticket lady, "Where is the gate for the plane that leaves for London?" She checked it out and said, "No plane leaves here tonight for London." I didn't realize it was a charter plane. I waited a bit.

Walking to a quiet place against the wall, I silently asked God for help. By and by, a man dressed in a bright, bronze-colored outfit spoke to me. He looked so regal. His posture gave him a look of authority.

As I leaned against the wall, I must have looked afraid and confused. He spoke to me, "Lady, can I help you?" I said, "My plane is going to London. I don't know how to get to the plane."

Right away, he gave me many directions to turn left, take the A train to a certain stop, take the elevator, catch train B, get off, somewhere, walk to another place, catch another train, get off at such and such a stop, see an elevator, get on that elevator, going up to the check-in place, then turn right, hurry from gate 4 to gate 14 to make it on time.

I thanked him. Then I dashed.

Starting toward the first train, I knew I did not remember all those trains and gates. But I did remember I had asked God for help. This man seemed so certain. Yet—time was getting cut too short. One train at a time. Finally, I got off that last train.

Right before me was an elevator. I entered, and the door shut behind me. All I saw was a tall piece of silver-looking metal. No buttons, just bare metal. Now I know God hears you when you whisper. But in my desperation, I screamed with all my voice, "GOD GET ME THERE!"

Then I moved a bit to the left. Ahh, there was the button! Up-elevator and into the check-out room. They slowly checked both suitcases. And I was free to flee. Down that corridor I flew. From gate 4 to gate 14 was a long, long way.

With ten minutes to spare, I checked in as the last person to board for London. Shirley looked relieved. I was shaking. All the way over the Atlantic Ocean, I thought of how close I had come to NOT going to London.

The man—as regal as he looked—I decided he was my own personal angel. The screaming to God was forgiven, as only God can. We were nearly in London when Shirley said, "I was just about to turn in my ticket. I did not want to be all alone in Europe for twenty-three days."

You know, I have asked the Lord for help so many times, and I find He is ALWAYS there. My trust in God deepens each time He answers so powerfully. Life experiences, as well as the Holy Scriptures, tell us about simply trusting God.

I can truly join with King David who said, "I will say of the Lord, He is my refuge and my fortress: my God; in him will I trust" (Ps. 91:2).

Lost in London

Shirley, my travelling companion, rolled her suitcase onto the train, just ahead of me. This was her seventh trip to England and Europe. She really knew her way around.

My suitcase, in the jostle of the crowd, had turned sideways, and I was trying to get it back on its wheels as I started to enter the train. Then, before I could pull the suitcase onto the train, the door closed. Half way in, half way out, the closing doors startled me, so I backed out. The train zoomed on.

As the train rushed on out of sight, I realized Shirley—my guide and protector—was gone. Frozen in fear for a few moments, I knew I needed to do the right thing. But what was that?

Because Shirley carried the money and had the tickets, I felt like I was a stranger in a foreign country, not even certain where north was. Walking back to our hotel was unthinkable. In my panic, I realized I couldn't even think of the name of our hotel.

In my mind, I knew I could not even ask for help. I was near hysteria when I remembered God. "HELP ME, GOD!" I screamed silently, my eyes wide open. No agonizing on my knees.

Just then, the next train arrived. The doors burst open. No one needed to say, "Hurry up!" I quickly pulled my suitcase inside THAT train. I wondered where this train would take me.

In my panic, I had forgotten my prayer. As I tried to form a plan, the train stopped. Looking out the door, to my great delight and relief, I spotted Shirley just a few feet beyond the door of the train.

Grabbing my suitcase, I exited the train and fell into her assuring arms. I blubbered, "I didn't know what to do." She snickered and said, "Well, you did the logical thing."

Logical? Perhaps, but did I thank God for helping me do "the next right thing?" Oh, no. I was back home in New Mexico before I said, "Thank You, Lord."

Why does it take me so long to say, "Thank you" when I'm so quick to demand, "HELP?"

Twenty-three gorgeous days in seven countries is a top memory in my long and adventurous life.

I join King David as he said in Psalm 116:1–2 (NIV): "I love the Lord, for he heard my voice; he heard my cry for mercy. Because he turned his ear to me, I will call on him as long as I live."

The Power of Music

"I have a headache. Could I be excused from my lesson today?" I don't know how many times over the last sixty years I have heard this excuse for skipping a piano lesson.

My response is, "Well, let's just play your favorite song first, then you can go." Nearly every time when these particular lessons are completed, I ask my student, "How is your headache?" Usually the response is, "What headache?"

Music has power. I love the Latin rhythms and calypso from Trinidad. I love the patriotic music of my own country—the good ol' USA. There are hymns and spiritual songs that cut deep in my soul, bringing an awareness of the presence of God.

For the most part, as a piano teacher, I love the great concert themes. I love the symphonies of Brahms and Beethoven. My delight is an evening with Mozart, Haydn, or Dvořák, to name a few. Music fills soul and body as nothing can.

Music therapy is a fairly new occupation. The more we study music, the more we find that mentally and physically handicapped people respond to music when nothing else can reach them. Children naturally clap and dance with tunes that are suitable for their age. Tears of the memories of religious experiences trickle down the cheeks of old-timers when someone sings, "Amazing Grace."

So music has capacity to lift the mood, to release the emotions, and even to change people for the better. Yet, there is danger in certain modern music. Once "rock music" became popular and progressively louder, its rhythm did not lead to higher and purer emotions. Not only the music, but the lyrics themselves lead us on a downward road. Elevating music

AND words are the best for us spiritually. But now—NOW—is the time to explore music with HIGHER themes, music that encourages a HIGHER level of thought, a HIGHER look at life. Try it. It never hurts to try a better grade of music. Who knows, maybe that headache will go away for you. (I'm just teasing, but there IS something to it.)

Don't forget that God is the Creator of music and that there is music in heaven! All music should be pleasing to Him. "I saw the redeemed host bow and cast their glittering crowns at the feet of Jesus, and then… they touched their golden harps and filled all heaven with their rich music and songs to the Lamb…."7 Music can also enhance your time with God. Psalm 81:1 says, "Sing aloud unto God our strength: make a joyful noise unto the God of Jacob."

God bless you as you reach for the best of everything you can, including the highest quality of music—music that is in tune with the songs of heaven!

We...

Jail is not just a place. It is more like an attitude. Many people in jail or prison glow with the presence of God. They glow because they have allowed the Holy Spirit into their lives. They have accepted Jesus Christ as their Savior.

Many people on death row feel God's Presence so close and so deeply in their hearts that they have no fear of death. How can this be?

Over 2,000 years ago, Jesus Himself gave us the secret to this glow. It is the assurance of life with God—no matter where we are in life.

Families and friends of those behind bars have their own "prison" also. A person does not have to be "locked up" to feel the intense emotions of isolation that life can bring.

By beholding we...Who is "We"? "We" is you. "We" is me. "We" is ALL of us. How can we be sure of that?

The secret of connecting with God and people is the first word in the Lord's Prayer: "OUR." When we pray "Our Father," we become connected with the human race, God's marvelous creatures—His creation, you and me—We.

As we pray these two words in the beginning of the Lord's prayer, we become connected with ALL of God's children. "Our Father" joins OUR hearts together—no one is left out. (The entire Lord's Prayer is found in Matthew 6:9–13.)

As we say, "Our Father," hatred is released. Jealousy vanishes. A new love flows through our hearts. Suddenly, WE realize WE are not alone. Because of Jesus's death on the cross for our sins, the Holy Spirit connects us with our heavenly Father. Our "God-spot" is filled. We are instantly complete. We are no longer alone.

Self-pity, self-sufficiency dissolves—the new need to share your new God-filled life with someone else becomes a new and instant experience. Many have this blessing. You can, too.

We are never alone. God is always there. Give God a chance. By Beholding, WE become changed.

The Perfect Christmas

When I was five years old, my uncle gave me a dolly for Christmas. I named her Annette. I loved that doll. A year later, Christmastime brought me another doll and a cradle that my Dad made for my dolls. Christmas was a happy family time. Five uncles, four grandparents, one brother, and a growing number of cousins completed my family. Every Christmas, we crowded into our small home.

The good-natured teasing and genuine laughter gave my brother and me great memories. When I was seven, I received skates. They were my new "getaway." I lived on those skates. Eight years into my life, Mom and Dad bought an old upright piano. My whole life changed that year. During my third piano lesson, I looked at my teacher and thought, I'm going to do what she's doing. I will be a piano teacher. It was a life-changing gift. I have taught piano lessons for 62 years now.

On my ninth Christmas, my piano teacher found a beautiful six-foot grand piano that just fit into our small living room. My future destiny was locked into place with that most thoughtful gift.

As I grew older, WW II started. My uncles joined the Navy or the Army. Christmas was filled with fear and absence. Never again did I have a truly jolly Christmas. However, the day left me with a longing for another perfect Christmas.

Years passed before I married. The man I married was a new Christian. But our Christmases were spent in taking care of his mom and dad in their drunken stupor. Or if we went to my parent's home, we were in grief because my brother's little boy had cystic fibrosis. All Christmas day was spent on hospital talk, with a profound sadness, and nearly no laughter at all.

When my nephew died at 10½ years of age, my mother declared, "Well, we will never again have Christmas." And in truth—we never did.

My husband, meanwhile, preferred his motorcycle and buddies to Christmas. The loneliness became nearly unbearable for me. When marriage finally turned too abusive for me to tolerate, I left. Then for many years I experienced my favorite holiday in a "solo" fashion. Friends were always nice to me, but I was alone—rarely to feel the Christmas joy that came naturally during all of my childhood.

Many years after my first marriage dissolved, I married again to a very loving man. Along the way, someone wisely told me, "Christmas is for children." I tried to let that longing go, but Christmas was locked into my DNA, and I kept the longing throughout the year. When I married again, I had longed for a mate AND a family, dreaming of Christmas JOY. That first Christmas was a "get-acquainted holiday," filled with laughter, TV, and gifts again. I was at peace with my new family. And I dreamed of wonderful Christmas days ahead.

So for Christmas 2016, I spent money on gifts, fully expecting to share the joy, laughter, and coziness of family. Well, it didn't happen. Two days before Christmas, my husband fell, hitting his head on the garage door, and he was in pain. So we called his daughter to pick up the gifts. We stayed alone in the house. We had leftovers for Christmas dinner. After lunch, my husband slept all day.

Christmases from long ago burst into my mind all day long. The intense loneliness finally drove me to my knees. I prayed for something to lift the dark mood that pressed down on me.

There on my knees, I discovered what Christmas is all about. Why did I not think of this before? Why did I feel so empty all these Christmases for years and years? As I was praying, a light bulb went on in my brain. Oh, all those years, I had "delighted" in gifts, laughter, relatives, friends, and food. But I left Christ out of Christmas. As a Christian who loves the Lord very much, I was shocked to realize what I had been doing. Now I know. Every day is now a PERFECT CHRISTMAS DAY, because a day with Jesus IS Christmas—every day.

King Jesus

THIS IS JESUS THE KING OF THE JEWS. The disciple, Matthew, was also author of the first book in the Gospels in the New Testament. He plainly states what was written over Jesus's head on the cross (Matt. 27:37).

The book of Mark calls "THE KING OF THE JEWS" a "...superscription of his accusation" (Mark 15:26). And Mark goes on to describe the people's reaction to His crucifixion: "Save thyself, and come down from the cross" (Mark 15:30).

The priests and scribes mocked: "...He saved others; himself he cannot save" (Mark 15:31).

Luke's wording of the same experience is, "THIS IS THE KING OF THE JEWS" (Luke 23:38), and he describes the rulers deriding Him.

The New International Version puts it this way: "...the rulers even sneered at him..., the soldiers also came up and mocked him. They offered him wine vinegar..." (Luke 23:35–36, NIV).

But Luke also tells of two important reactions in men who saw Jesus as truly their KING. The thief hanging on a cross saw his KING dying for his sins. He recognized Jesus as his Savior and said, "...Jesus, remember me when you come into your kingdom" (Luke 23:42, NIV). Also, the centurion recognized Jesus as a King. "Now when the centurion saw what was done, he glorified God, saying, Certainly this was a righteous man" (Luke 23:47).

John was Jesus's closest disciple and the author of the Gospel of John. He was standing near the cross. He had this to say about Jesus being described as "KING" in John 19:19–23, giving us a picture of just how important the superscription above Jesus's head was.

It was Pilate, the Roman Governor of Judea, who wrote a title and put it on the cross: "And the writing was JESUS OF NAZARETH THE KING OF THE JEWS" (John 19:19). He wrote it in Hebrew, and Greek, and Latin. The Jewish chief priests tried to get Pilate to write that "HE SAID I am King of the Jews." Pilate answered the priests: "What I have written I have written" (John 19:21–22) (emphasis added).

The thief, the centurion, and even Pilate, the Roman governor, saw in Jesus the truth that JESUS IS KING.

When Jesus died, the devil was happy. The Jewish leaders were happy. But the disciples were disappointed and extremely sad and afraid. Even Mary, Jesus's mother, didn't understand about the importance of the cross. She went away crying. But that was Friday, the darkest day on earth.

As a Christian, I'm always happy when I think about MY KING on the first day of the week. HE ROSE FROM THE GRAVE—a victorious Savior! He gave the victory to all of us, if we want it—victory over ALL sin. And a promise to live with Him forever in His home: Heaven. It will take a long time to thank Him for dying on that cross. And I'm glad He promises eternal life to us. The cross and the superscription on that cross state the TRUTH: JESUS IS THE KING. And He will be forever and ever.

The very same Pilate who asked, "What is truth?" (John 18:38), told the truth: JESUS IS KING.

Be What You Ought to Be

Someone has noted that every moment of our lives, we should be what we ought to be because one person can make a difference. That means being the best that God has in mind for us spiritually.

Leaning on the Lord for overcoming our weaknesses is the very best way to "be what I ought to be." And if one person really can make a difference in this world then I realize that I should at least try, with God's help to be that person.

Yes, all day I'm doing several things that really can make a difference, and yet, there is always room for more. Just now, as I'm thinking and writing as I think—I realize that PRAYING for YOU, my dear reader, is something that really can make a difference. So, YOU, my reader—will be in my heart and prayers all day long as I go from event to event. I truly hope you feel the POWER OF PRAYER.

As a day ends and evening brings quietness, I feel grateful for another day of life. Because life is the most important thing we have. And only God can give us the gift of life. So my heart turns to my Creator. I've been thanking Him for even thinking about me—long, long ago for giving me my own special life. I realize that each one of us has that blessing.

God gives us incredible forgiveness for our blunders, our rebellion, and our out-and-out sins. I'm just grateful that loving us and forgiving us is all part of the character of God. Only Jesus was perfect. That's a relief to me. Trying to be good on any given day seems useless, sometimes even hopeless. But, at the end of any day, it is good to turn to God, thanking Him for protection and forgiveness, comfort and closeness. Trying to be what I ought to be and trying to make a difference in other's lives seems to be a big challenge. But with God's help, each day has its very special spot. It's that part that I cherish before I go to bed for a good rest at night.

Sometimes I go to bed with a good clean conscience. Other times I lie awake and ponder the day I just lived. It's so very good to know that God is right there, even if things did not go exactly right that day. The Spirit of God is always with us. He is the presence of the Lord. Even though we do not see Him, Jesus has promised His Spirit as a constant companion, all the time, every day, anywhere. "...Lo, I am with you..." (Matt. 28:20).

I love you, dear reader. I hope the very best day for you is TODAY and all your todays after that.

Clouds

When Job was covered with boils, his three "friends" talked to him. One friend, Elihu, challenged Job: "Listen to this, Job; stop and consider God's wonders. Do you know how God controls the clouds and makes his lightening flash? Do you know how the clouds hang poised—those wonders of him who is perfect in knowledge?" (Job 37:14–17, NIV).

When I moved from Arizona to Nebraska, my good friend, Merilyn, assured me that the sun still shines but that it's shining above the clouds. Since I was born in San Diego, moved to Northern California in my teen years, and traveled and worked in Arizona and New Mexico, I found Nebraska's skies so different. And on many days, "cloud cover" is just that—a "cover" of clouds.

King David observed, "The heavens declare the glory of God" (Ps. 19:1). Sun, moon, and stars speak of God's great power. In a different way, the clouds in our atmosphere also bring our attention to the "glory of God."

When the good man, Job, lost all his possessions, his family, and then suffered from boils—from head to toe—he finally challenged God. The Lord answered back: "Where were you when I laid the earth's foundation?" (Job 38:4, NIV). God wants to know where was Job when He made the clouds and all the long list of mighty works showing His power and creative genius.

In so many ways, clouds declare, and will declare, the glory of God. In the wilderness, God protected His people for forty years with a cloud by day. And to keep them warm on those chilly desert nights, He sent a "pillar of fire" (Exod. 13:21) to keep them warm.

A cloud covered Moses on the mountain, as he received the Ten Commandments from God (Exod. 19:16).

Jesus Himself ascended in a cloud toward His heavenly home soon after His resurrection (Acts 1:9). And we have the promise He shall return in "clouds of heaven with power and great glory" (Matt. 24:30, Rev. 1:7). This is our great promise of hope—the experience that all God's people pray for. He IS returning soon.

To the many people who argue, "I don't want to sit on a cloud and play the harp all day:" I agree. But not to worry. Heaven is a real city with real homes for each of us (John 14:2).

Years ago, on the lowest day of my life, the Lord gave me my own personal cloud. I took a walk to help ease the hurt. By and by, I sat on a bench and looked up. A large black cloud filled a huge portion of the western sky. I have seen many grey clouds, but this was the only black cloud I had ever seen. Completely surrounding the black cloud was a golden brilliance. Indeed, behind the cloud was the setting sun. I like to think the Spirit of God was there, too—giving me the assurance that He knew where I was in life.

Yes, He knows our address. He knows where we live. He knows our hurt. He is a personal God who cares, who touches us right where we are with His incredible love.

Consider the clouds.

Failed, but Not a Failure

We have all failed some part of our lives. Some failures put us behind bars. But the Creator, who created you, looks down and says, "You have failed, but YOU, My child, are NOT a failure."

Just last week, I failed. Not once, not twice, but three times. It brought back to my mind the "F" I received in algebra when I was young. I can remember handing my report card to my dad. (Mom would have paddled my behind.) I remember Dad looking up and down my grade card. His eyes stopped at the "F." As he glanced over to the left, he said, "Algebra." My heart nearly stopped.

> *We have all failed some part of our lives. Some failures put us behind bars. But the Creator, who created you, looks down and says, "You have failed, but YOU, My child, are NOT a failure."*

Then after a long, long pause, he took a deep breath and said, "Well, next year we will study algebra every night together right after supper. And we did. Each night, after dishes, he explained the assignment for that day. So many times I said, "Dad, it's impossible," but Dad encouraged me, and I would just try once more. That school year, I got a "B" grade. Dad understood my non-mathematical mind. Because of his love and help, I knew algebra was at first my failure. But I, myself, was NOT the failure.

Now, as an old lady, I had failed again. I needed my driver's license. But I could not "get the hang of" the computer questions. I got so nervous, I answered questions stupidly—and failed. After a little coaching at the computer in the library, I returned to take the test again. And I passed. Phew!!!

Then came the vision test. For some reason, I could not focus on the very small letters and numbers, and I flunked again. This time, yes, I could drive in the daytime, but not at night. Partially failing this test meant that I would have to find a nighttime driver to go to work. Going home in the dark three nights every week, I would need help from three friends who COULD drive at night.

The next day, as I was taking the driving test in the car, I failed once more. UGH! Walking out of that office, I was totally stripped of my self-worth.

As I was walking out into the lobby, I bumped into a friend.

"What happened, Joy?" he asked. "I just flunked three driving tests," I blurted out.

"Oh, you just failed three tests. That does not mean YOU are a failure." Those kind words gave me the courage to try again the next day. And knowing I'm not a failure, I pulled on a "garment of courage" and passed the driving test.

We have all failed some part of our lives. Some failures put us behind bars. But the Creator, who created you, looks down and says, "You have failed a test, but YOU, My child, are NOT a failure."

And 1 John 1:9 says, "If we confess our sins, he is faithful and just to forgive us our sins, and to cleanse us from all unrighteousness."

My friend, we all have a Friend in heaven just waiting to forgive our sins. Talk to Him, your Creator, and tell Him about your failures. Ask forgiveness and be very certain of this: YOU ARE NOT A FAILURE!

Christians are not perfect people—they are just forgiven.

Embrace Solitude

We humans fear being alone. Yet, once we have discovered "alone-ness," we wrap our arms about it. Don't we all love watching a large family at the table, telling stories, laughing, telling secrets, just having a good time loving life together?

Yet, for the most part, most of us find ourselves ALONE a lot. Larger families are fractured into small groups and move apart from each other. Telephones, even computers and cell phones, are just not the same as being together in the same room.

Taking alone time further, being behind bars brings on a special kind of alone-ness that is difficult at first. However, there are many people who discover the closeness of their Creator in the middle of all the noise. Poets, artists, and composers spend most of their creative time alone. Yet, we all crave closeness to others.

Spending much time living and working all alone, I have discovered a certain kind of satisfaction in solitude. It seems that quiet times give a person a chance to talk with our Creator God and to allow Him to impress us with His thoughts. And this is just what Jesus did while He lived on earth over two thousand years ago. Before the sun came up, Jesus was on His knees talking with His Father. He talked with God as He walked up the hill to meet privately with His Father—to talk aloud without being embarrassed by others or interrupted. He deliberately choose SOLITUDE.

Once we quit running from ourselves, get calm, allow our inner spirit to catch up with our speeding body, and stand still, we can finally become aware of God's presence in that most special way. As we allow Him to wrap His arms of LOVE around us, a stillness fills us with the true LIFE we all long for. Even in a crowded room, that wonderful stillness of the presence of God calms our spirits—even gives us JOY.

Too many times, we say, I'm not good enough for God. But that's why Jesus died. No one is "Good enough" for God. But on the cross, Jesus Himself took care of that problem. Because He died for our sins (all sin, including the worst that can be imagined), we are safe to fall into His arms and allow His life to recharge our lives. Within the very name of Jesus is the meaning, "For he shall SAVE His people from their sins" (Matt. 1:21) (emphasis added). He is OUR Savior. Grateful, needy, in a way pitiful, but we can talk with Him any time, all the time.

Give God a try. Give Him a chance to show you the enormous blessings of solitude. That "alone time with God—you will find that you want it more and more. I do.

Jesus IS in Jail

I was talking to three female inmates a few months ago, and they all glowed with the presence of the Lord. Their faces actually shone. They all expressed that, "Jesus is in jail." We had a long talk about their future.

Each girl had a different story, of course. One was to get out of jail the following week. Being the teacher I am, I couldn't help asking what she was going to do once the last prison door clanged behind her, and she was outside. She laughed and said, "I have no plans."

We talked quite a while. I expressed that, for her, Jesus was in jail, but did she expect to take Him with her in the outside world or leave Him behind? Grabbing her Bible, she said, "This I will take with me." She had learned to pray and had a strong conviction that God would lead, no matter her past, but she wasn't sure where she wanted to go. Finally, she said, "I do have an aunt in California who loves me and believes in me. She told me to come any time. I'll call her and go to her home."

The second girl was going to be in jail for a bit longer, so she had more time to think about her future once she would get out. We also talked quite a bit. Her family didn't want her, but she had a degree and felt certain she could get a job.

The third girl was the one most aglow with the Lord's presence. She said, "I have my trial next week. They either will let me go free, or I will be sent to the penitentiary for twenty years."

I swallowed hard and asked, "Either way, do you plan to take Jesus with you?"

Her reply was encouraging to me. She said, "Either way, God will be my God no matter what. I have no fear."

Some of you who are reading this book will be out of jail soon. I'll ask you, too: "Do you have a plan?"

I wrote this book because I really care about you, but Jesus cares a whole lot more than I ever could. Jesus created you, redeemed your life on the cross, and is coming back very soon—sooner than we think.

Now is the time to fall on your knees and say, "God, I need a Savior." Ask God for Jesus. It can't hurt, but it can heal. May God always bless you!

Bibliography

1. White, Ellen G. *Patriarchs and Prophets.* Washington, DC: Review and Herald Publishing Association, 1890, 218.3.

2. White, Ellen G. *Prophets and Kings.* Mountain View, CA: Pacific Press Publishing Association, 1917, 542.1.

3. White, Ellen G. *The Desire of Ages.* Mountain View, CA: Pacific Press Publishing Association, 1898, 713.3.

4. *The American Heritage Dictionary of the English Language.* Boston: Houghton Mifflin, 2000.

5. Taylor, Ida Scott. *The Year Book of American Authors.* New York: Raphael Tuck and Sons, 1894, 109.

6. White, Ellen G. *The Desire of Ages.* Mountain View, CA: Pacific Press Publishing Association, 1898, 636.1.

7. White, Ellen G. *Early Writings.* Washington, DC: Review and Herald Publishing Association, 1882, 288.1.

www.ingramcontent.com/pod-product-compliance
Lightning Source LLC
Chambersburg PA
CBHW060551100426
42742CB00013B/2520